THE DiViNE MATRIX

Also by Gregg Braden

Books

Awakening to Zero Point*
The God Code
The Isaiah Effect*
Secrets of the Lost Mode of Prayer
The Spontaneous Healing of Belief (available November 2007)
Walking Between the Worlds*

CD Programs

An Ancient Magical Prayer (with Deepak Chopra)
Awakening the Power of a Modern God
The Divine Name (with Jonathan Goldman)
The Gregg Braden Audio Collection*
Speaking the Lost Language of God
The Spontaneous Healing of Belief (available November 2007)
Unleashing the Power of the God Code

*All the above are available from Hay House
except items marked with an asterisk

Please visit Hay House USA: **www.hayhouse.com**
Hay House Australia: **www.hayhouse.com.au**
Hay House UK: **www.hayhouse.co.uk**
Hay House South Africa: **orders@psdprom.co.za**
Hay House India: **www.hayhouseindia.co.in**

THE DiViNE MATRIX

BRiDGiNG TiME, SPACE, MiRACLES, AND BELiEF

Gregg Braden

HAY HOUSE, INC.
Carlsbad, California
London • Sydney • Johannesburg
Vancouver • Hong Kong • New Delhi

Published and distributed in the United States by: Hay House, Inc.: www. hayhouse.com • *Published and distributed in Australia by:* Hay House Australia Pty. Ltd.: www.hayhouse.com.au • *Published and distributed in the United Kingdom by:* Hay House UK, Ltd.: www.hayhouse.co.uk • *Published and distributed in the Republic of South Africa by:* Hay House SA (Pty), Ltd.: orders@psdprom.co.za • *Distributed in Canada by:* Raincoast: www.raincoast. com • *Published in India by:* Hay House Publications (India) Pvt. Ltd.: www. hayhouseindia.co.in

Editorial consultation: Stephanie Gunning • *Editorial supervision:* Jill Kramer
Design: Suzie Bergstrom

Grateful acknowledgment is made to the Institute of HeartMath for permission to reprint the illustration in Figure 2, to Christopher Logue for permission to reprint his poem "Come to the Edge" in the Introduction, and to Alvin Lee and Chrysalis Music Group for permission to reprint the excerpt from "I'd Love to Change the World" in Chapter 8.

Library of Congress Cataloging-in-Publication Data

Braden, Gregg.
  The divine matrix: bridging time, space, miracles, and belief / Gregg Braden.
    p. cm.
  Includes bibliographical references and index.
  ISBN-13: 978-1-4019-0570-5 (hardcover)
  ISBN-13: 978-1-4019-0573-6 (tradepaper) 1. Spirituality. I. Title.
  BL624.B632 2007
  299'.93—dc22   2006019660

Hardcover: ISBN: 978-1-4019-0570-5
Tradepaper: ISBN: 978-1-4019-0573-6

10 09 08 07   5 4 3 2
1st edition, January 2007
2nd edition, January 2007

Printed in the United States of America

CONTENTS

I have one small drop
of knowing in my soul.
Let it dissolve in your ocean.

— Rumi

"All matter originates and exists only by virtue of a force. . . .
We must assume behind this force the existence
of a conscious and intelligent Mind.
This Mind is the <u>matrix</u> of all matter."

— Max Planck, 1944

With these words, Max Planck, the father of quantum
theory, described a universal field of energy that
connects everything in creation: *the Divine Matrix.*

The Divine Matrix *is* our world.
It is also everything *in* our world.
It is us and all that we love, hate, create, and experience.
Living in the Divine Matrix, we are as artists expressing
our innermost passions, fears, dreams, and desires
through the essence of a mysterious quantum canvas.
But *we are* the canvas, as well as the images upon the canvas.
We are the paints, as well as the brushes.

In the Divine Matrix, we are the container
within which all things exist, the bridge between
the creations of our inner and outer worlds,
and the mirror that shows us what we have created.

This book is written for those of you who long to awaken
the power of your greatest passions and deepest aspirations.
In the Divine Matrix, you are the seed of the miracle,
as well as the miracle itself.

INTRODUCTION

Come to the edge.
We might fall.
Come to the edge.
It's too high!
COME TO THE EDGE
And they came.
and he pushed.
and they flew.

With these words, we're shown a beautiful example of the power that awaits us when we allow ourselves to venture beyond the bounds of what we've always believed to be true in our lives. In this brief dialogue from the contemporary poet Christopher Logue, a group of initiates find themselves in an experience that's very different from what they had originally expected.[1] Rather than simply being *at* the edge, through their teacher's encouragement, they find themselves *beyond* it, in a way that's both surprising and empowering. It is in this uncharted territory that they experience themselves in a new way—and in their discovery, they find a new freedom.

In many respects, the pages that follow are like coming to the initiates' edge. They describe the existence of a field of energy—the Divine Matrix—that provides the container, as well as a bridge and a mirror, for everything that happens between the world within us and the one outside of our bodies. The fact that this field exists in everything from the smallest particles of the quantum atom to distant galaxies whose light is just now reaching our eyes, and in everything between, changes what we've believed about our role in creation.

For some of you, what you're about to read is a new and very different way of thinking about how things work in life. For others, it's a comforting synthesis of what you already know, or at least suspect, to be true. For everyone, however, the existence of a primal web of energy that connects your bodies, the world, and everything in the universe opens the door to a powerful and mysterious possibility.

That possibility suggests that we may be much more than simply observers passing through a brief moment of time in a creation that already exists. When we look at "life"—our spiritual and material abundance, our relationships and careers, our deepest loves and greatest achievements, along with our fears and the lack of all these things—we may also be gazing squarely in the mirror of our truest, and sometimes most unconscious, beliefs. We see them in our surroundings because they're made manifest through the mysterious essence of the Divine Matrix, and for this to be the case, *consciousness itself* must play a key role in the existence of the universe.

WE ARE THE ARTISTS AS WELL AS THE ART

As far-fetched as this idea may sound to many people, it is precisely at the crux of some of the greatest controversies among some of the most brilliant minds in recent history. In a quote from his autobiographical notes, for example, Albert Einstein shared his belief that we're essentially passive observers living in a universe already in place, one in which we seem to have little influence: "Out yonder there was this huge world," he said, "which exists independently of us human beings and which stands before us like a great, eternal riddle, at least partially accessible to our inspection and thinking."[2]

In contrast to Einstein's perspective, which is still widely held by many scientists today, John Wheeler, a Princeton physicist and colleague of Einstein, offers a radically different view of our role in creation. In terms that are bold, clear, and graphic, Wheeler says, "We had this old idea, that there was a universe *out there,* [author's emphasis] and here is man, the observer, safely protected from the universe by a six-inch slab of plate glass." Referring to the late-20th-century experiments that show us how simply looking at something *changes* that something, Wheeler continues, "Now we learn from the quantum world that even to observe so minuscule an object as an electron we have to shatter that plate glass: we have to reach in there. . . . So the old word *observer* simply has to be crossed off the books, and we must put in the new word *participator.*"[3]

What a shift! In a radically different interpretation of our relationship to the world we live in, Wheeler states that it's impossible for us to simply watch the universe happen around us. Experiments in quantum physics, in fact, do show that simply looking at something as tiny as an electron—just focusing our awareness upon what it's doing for even an instant in time—changes its properties while we're watching it. The experiments suggest that the very act of observation is an act of creation, and that consciousness is doing the creating. These findings seem to support Wheeler's proposition that we can no longer consider ourselves merely onlookers who have no effect on the world that we're observing.

To think of ourselves as participating in creation rather than simply passing through the universe during the brief period of a lifetime requires a new perception of what the cosmos is and how it works. The groundwork for such a radical worldview was the basis for a series of books and papers by another Princeton physicist and colleague of Einstein, David Bohm. Before his death in 1992, Bohm left us two pioneering theories that offer a very different—and in some ways, a nearly holistic—view of the universe and our role in it.

The first was an interpretation of quantum physics that set the stage for Bohm's meeting and subsequent friendship with Einstein. It was this theory that opened the door to what Bohm called the "creative operation of underlying . . . levels of reality."[4] In other words, he believed that there are deeper or higher planes of creation that hold the template for what happens in our world. It's from these subtler levels of reality that our physical world originates.

His second theory was an explanation of the universe as a single unified system of nature, connected in ways that aren't always obvious. During his early work at the University of California's Lawrence Radiation Laboratory (now Lawrence Livermore National Laboratory), Bohm had the opportunity to observe small particles of atoms in a special gaseous state called *plasma*. Bohm found that when the particles were in this plasma state, they behaved less like the individual units that we typically think of and more like they were connected to one another as part of a greater existence. These experiments laid the foundation for the pioneering work for which Bohm is probably best remembered—his 1980 book, *Wholeness and the Implicate Order.*

In this paradigm-shifting volume, Bohm proposed that if we could see the universe in its entirety from a higher vantage point, the objects in our world would in fact appear as a projection of things happening in another realm that we cannot observe. He viewed both the seen as well as the unseen as expressions of a greater, more universal order. To distinguish between them, he called these two realms "implicate" and "explicate."

The things that we can see and touch and that appear separate in our world—such as rocks, oceans, forests, animals, and people— are examples of the *explicate order* of creation. However, as distinct as they may appear from one another, Bohm suggested that they're linked in a deeper reality in ways that we simply cannot see from our place in creation. He viewed all of the things that look separate to us as part of a greater wholeness, which he called the *implicate order.*

To describe the difference between implicate and explicate, he gave the analogy of a flowing stream. Using the different ways we can see water flowing in the same stream as a metaphor, Bohm described the illusion of separateness: "On this stream, one may see an ever-changing pattern of vortices, ripples, waves, splashes, etc., which evidently have no independent existence as such."[5] Although the water's disturbances may look separate to us, Bohm viewed them as intimately linked and deeply connected to one another. "Such transitory subsistence as may be possessed by these abstracted forms *implies only a relative independence* [author's emphasis] rather than absolutely independent existence," he stated.[6] In other words, they're all part of the same water.

Bohm used such examples to describe his sense that the universe and everything in it—including us—may, in fact, be part of a grand cosmic pattern where all portions are evenly shared by every other. Encapsulating this unified view of nature, Bohm simply stated, "The new form of insight can perhaps best be called *Undivided Wholeness in Flowing Movement*."[7]

In the 1970s, Bohm offered an even clearer metaphor to describe how the universe may be thought of as a distributed yet undivided whole. Reflecting on the interrelated nature of creation, he became more convinced that the universe works like a grand cosmic hologram. In a hologram, every portion of whatever the object is contains that object in its entirety, only on a smaller scale. (For those who may be unfamiliar with the concept of a hologram, a detailed explanation is provided in Chapter 4.) From Bohm's perspective, what we see as our world is actually the projection of something even more real that's happening at a deeper level of creation. It is this deeper level that's the original— the implicate. In this view of "As above, so below" and "As within, so without," patterns are contained within patterns, complete in and of themselves and different only in scale.

The elegant simplicity of the human body offers us a beautiful example of a hologram, one that's already familiar. The DNA from any part of our bodies contains our genetic code—the entire pattern of DNA—for the rest of the body, no matter where it comes from. Whether we sample our hair, a fingernail, or our blood, the genetic pattern that makes us who we are is always there in the code . . . it's always the same.

Just as the universe is constantly changing from implicate to explicate, the flow from the unseen to the seen is what makes up the dynamic current of creation. It's this constantly changing nature of creation that John Wheeler had in mind when he described the universe as "participatory"—that is, unfinished and continually responding to consciousness.

Interestingly, this is precisely the way that the wisdom traditions of the past suggest that our world works. From the ancient Indian Vedas, believed by some scholars to date to 5,000 B.C., to the 2,000-year-old Dead Sea Scrolls, a general theme seems to suggest that the world is actually the mirror of things that are happening on a higher realm or in a deeper reality. For example, commenting on the new translations of the Dead Sea Scroll fragments known as *The Songs of the Sabbath Sacrifice,* its translators summarize the content: "What happens on earth is but a pale reflection of that greater, ultimate reality."[8]

The implication of both quantum theory and the ancient texts is that in the unseen realms we create the blueprint for the relationships, careers, successes, and failures of the visible world. From this perspective, the Divine Matrix works like a great cosmic screen that allows us to see the nonphysical energy of our emotions and beliefs (our anger, hate, and rage; as well as our love, compassion, and understanding) projected in the physical medium of life.

Just as a movie screen reflects without judgment the image of whatever or whoever has been filmed, the Matrix appears to provide an unbiased surface for our inner experiences and beliefs to be seen in the world. Sometimes consciously, oftentimes not, we "show" our truest beliefs about everything from compassion to betrayal through the quality of relationships that surround us.

In other words, we're like artists expressing our deepest passions, fears, dreams, and desires through the living essence of a mysterious quantum canvas. However, unlike a conventional painter's canvas, which exists in one place at a given time, our canvas is the same stuff that everything is made of—it is everywhere and is always present.

Let's carry the artist/canvas analogy one step further. Traditionally, artists are separate from their work and use their tools to convey an inner creation through an outer expression. Within the Divine Matrix, however, the separation between art and artist disappears:

We *are* the canvas, as well as the images upon it; we *are* the tools, as well as the artist using them.

The very idea of us creating from within our own creation brings to mind one of those Walt Disney cartoons that were common on black-and-white television back in the '50s and '60s. We would first see the hand of an unidentified artist sketch a well-known cartoon character such as Mickey Mouse on a drawing pad. As the image was being formed, it would suddenly become animated and lifelike. Then Mickey would begin to create his own drawings of other cartoon characters *from within* the sketch itself. Suddenly, the original artist was no longer needed and out of the picture . . . literally.

With the hand nowhere to be seen, Mickey and his friends would take on lives and personalities of their own. While everyone in the make-believe house was sleeping, the entire kitchen would become joyously animated. As the sugar bowl danced with the saltshaker and the teacup rocked the world of the butter dish, the characters no longer had any connection to the artist. While this may be an oversimplification of how we function in the Divine Matrix, it also helps anchor the subtle and abstract idea of us as creators, creating from within our own creations.

Just as artists refine an image until it's exactly right in their minds, in many respects it appears that through the Divine Matrix we do the same thing with our life experiences. Through our palette of beliefs, judgments, emotions, and prayers, we find ourselves in relationships, jobs, and situations of support and betrayal that play out with different individuals in various places. At the same time, these people and situations often feel hauntingly familiar.

Both as individuals and together, we share our inner-life creations as a never-ending cycle of moment layered upon moment, day after day, and so on. What a beautiful, bizarre, and powerful concept! Just the way a painter uses the same canvas again and again while searching for the perfect expression of an idea, we may think of ourselves as perpetual artists, building a creation that's ever-changing and without end.

The implications of being surrounded by a malleable world of our own making are vast, powerful, and, to some, perhaps a little frightening. Our ability to use the Divine Matrix intentionally and creatively suddenly empowers us to alter everything about the way we see our role in the universe. At the very least, it suggests that there's much more to life than chance happenings and occasional synchronicities that we deal with the best we can.

Ultimately, our relationship to the quantum essence that connects us to everything else reminds us that we're creators ourselves. As such, we may express our deepest desires for healing, abundance, joy, and peace in everything from our bodies and lives to our relationships. And we may do so consciously, in the time and manner that we choose.

However, just as the initiates in Christopher Logue's poem at the beginning of this Introduction needed a little "nudge" to get them to fly, all of these possibilities require a subtle yet powerful shift in the way we think about our world and ourselves. In that shift, our secret desires, highest goals, and loftiest dreams suddenly appear within our grasp. As miraculous as such a reality may sound, all of these things—and much more—are possible within the realm of the Divine Matrix. The key is not only to understand how it works; we also need a language to communicate our desires that's recognizable to this ancient web of energy.

Our oldest and most cherished wisdom traditions remind us that there is, in fact, a language that speaks to the Divine Matrix, one that has no words and doesn't involve the usual outward signs of communication we make with our hands or body. It comes in a form so simple that we all already know how to "speak" it fluently. In fact, we use it every day of our lives—it is the language of human emotion.

Modern science has discovered that through each emotion we experience in our bodies, we also undergo chemical changes of things such as pH and hormones that mirror our feelings.[9] Through the "positive" experiences of love, compassion, and forgiveness and the "negative" emotions of hate, judgment, and jealousy, we each possess the power to affirm or deny our existence at each moment of every day. Additionally, the same emotion that gives us such power *within* our bodies extends this force into the quantum world *beyond* our bodies.

It may be helpful to think of the Divine Matrix as a cosmic blanket that begins and ends in the realm of the unknown and spans everything between. This covering is many layers deep and is everywhere all the time, already in place. Our bodies, lives, and all that we know exist and take place within its fibers. From our watery creation in our mother's womb to our marriages, divorces, friendships, and careers, all that we experience may be thought of as "wrinkles" in the blanket.

From a quantum perspective, everything from the atoms of matter and a blade of grass to our bodies, the planet, and beyond may be thought of as a "disturbance" in the smooth fabric of this space-time blanket. Perhaps it's no coincidence then that ancient spiritual and poetic traditions describe existence in much the same way. The Vedas, for example, speak of a unified field of "pure consciousness" that bathes and permeates all of creation.[10] In these traditions, our experiences of thought, feeling, emotion, and belief—and all the judgment that they create—are viewed as *disturbances,* interruptions in a field that is otherwise smooth and motionless.

In a similar fashion, the sixth-century *Hsin-Hsin Ming* (which translates to Faith-Mind Verses) describes the properties of an essence that is the blueprint for everything in creation. Called the Tao, it's ultimately beyond description, just as we see in the Vedic scriptures. It is all that is—the container of all experience, as well as the experience itself. The Tao is described as perfect, "like vast space where nothing is lacking and nothing is in excess."[11]

According to the *Hsin-Hsin Ming,* it's only when we disturb the tranquility of the Tao through our judgments that its harmony eludes us. When this inevitably does happen and we find ourselves enmeshed in feelings of anger and separation, the text offers guidelines to remedy this condition: "To come directly into harmony with this reality, just simply say when doubt arises, 'Not two.' In this 'not two' nothing is separate, nothing is excluded."[12]

While I admit that thinking of ourselves as a disturbance in the Matrix may take some of the romance out of life, it also gives us a powerful way to conceptualize our world and ourselves. If, for example, we want to form new, healthy, and life-affirming relationships; let healing romance into our lives; or bring a peaceful solution to the Middle East, we must create a new disturbance in the field, one that mirrors our desire. We must make a new "wrinkle" in the stuff that space, time, our bodies, and the world are made of.

This is our relationship to the Divine Matrix. We're given the power to imagine, dream, and feel life's possibilities from within the Matrix itself so that it can reflect back to us what we've created. Both ancient traditions and modern science have described how this cosmic mirror works; in the case of the experiments that will be shared in later chapters, we're even shown how these reflections work in the language of science. Admittedly, while these studies may solve some mysteries of creation, they also open the door to even deeper questions about our existence.

We clearly don't know all there is to know about the Divine Matrix. Science doesn't have all of the answers—in all honesty, scientists aren't even certain where the Divine Matrix came from, and we're also aware that we could study it for another hundred years and still not find all the answers. What we do know, however, is that the Divine Matrix exists. It is here, and we may tap its creative power through the language of our emotions.

We can apply this knowing in a way that's useful and meaningful in our lives. By doing so, our connection to one another and all things cannot be denied. It's in light of this connection that we may realize just how powerful we really are. From the place of strength that such a realization offers, we have the opportunity to become more peaceful and compassionate people, actively working to create a world that mirrors these qualities—and more. Through the Divine Matrix, we have the opportunity to focus on these attributes in our lives, applying them as our inner technology of feelings, imagination, and dreams. When we do, we tap the true essence of the power to change our lives and the world.

ABOUT THIS BOOK

In many respects, our experience of the Divine Matrix may be compared to the software that runs a computer. In both, the instructions must use a language that the system understands. For the computer, this is a numerical code of 0s and 1s. For consciousness, a different kind of language is required, one that uses no numbers, alphabets, or even words. Because we're already part of the Divine Matrix, it makes perfect sense that we would already have everything we need to communicate with it, without the need for an instruction manual or special training. And we do.

The language of consciousness appears to be the universal experience of emotion. We already know how to love, hate, fear, and forgive. Recognizing that these feelings are actually the instructions that program the Divine Matrix, we can hone our skills to better understand how to bring joy, healing, and peace to our lives.

This book isn't intended to be a definitive work on the history of science and the new physics. There are a number of other texts that have already done a wonderful job of bringing this kind of information to our awareness today. Some of them I have even referenced here—Michio Kaku's *Hyperspace,* for example, and David Bohm's *Wholeness and the Implicate Order.* Each of these represents a powerful new way to see our world, and I recommend them all.

This book is intended to be a useful tool—a guide—that we can apply to the mysteries of our everyday lives. For this reason, there are places where I've chosen to focus more on the radical and unexpected results of the quantum experiments, rather than getting bogged down with too many technical details of the experiments themselves. For us to understand the power to manifest healing, peace, joy, romance, and partnership, as well as to survive our time in history, it's important to emphasize what the results tell us about ourselves, rather than the fine points of how the studies were performed. For those who may be interested in the technical details, I've included the sources as endnotes.

For so many people, the breakthroughs in the world of quantum physics are little more than interesting facts—things to talk about at conferences or workshops or over a Starbucks latte. Yet, as deep as the implications go and as high as the philosophy carries us, the discoveries seem to have minimal relevance in our everyday lives. What good does it do, for example, to know that a particle of matter can be in two places at once or that electrons can travel faster than Einstein said they could if this knowledge doesn't add to our lives in some way? It's only when we can connect these mind-boggling discoveries to the healing of our bodies or to what we experience in the malls, living rooms, airports, and classrooms of our lives that they become important to us.

This apparent chasm between the mysteries of the quantum world and our everyday experiences is where *The Divine Matrix* offers a bridge. In addition to describing the findings, this book takes us one step further: It gives meaning to how those discoveries can help us become better people and build a better world together.

I've written this book for one reason: to offer a sense of hope, possibility, and empowerment in a world that often makes us feel small, ineffective, and helpless. And my goal is to do so in a conversational style that describes the awesome insights of the new science in a way that's easy to understand and interesting.

My experience with live presentations has shown that in order to reach an audience in a way that's meaningful, it's important to honor the way the listeners learn. Regardless of how "left-brained" we think we are or how "right-brained" we feel we are, the fact is that we all use both sides to make sense of the world. And while some people certainly do rely more on one hemisphere or the other, it's important to honor both our intuition as well as our logic when we invite people to make a huge leap in how they see the world.

For this reason, *The Divine Matrix* is written in much the same way that the fabric of a tapestry is created. Throughout these pages, I've woven the "right-brain" descriptions of personal accounts and direct experience into the "left-brain" research and reports of discoveries that tell us why these stories are important. This way of sharing information makes the data seem less textbooklike, while still keeping enough of the leading-edge science to make it meaningful.

Just as all life is built from the four chemical bases that create our DNA, the universe appears to be founded upon four characteristics of the Divine Matrix that make things work in the way they do. The key to tapping the power of the Matrix lies in our ability to embrace the four landmark discoveries that link it to our lives in an unprecedented way:

Discovery 1: There is a field of energy that connects all of creation.

Discovery 2: This field plays the role of a container, a bridge, and a mirror for the beliefs within us.

Discovery 3: The field is nonlocal and holographic. Every part of it is connected to every other, and each piece mirrors the whole on a smaller scale.

Discovery 4: We communicate with the field through the language of emotion.

It's our power to recognize and apply these realities that determine everything from our healing to the success of our relationships and careers. Ultimately, our survival as a species may be directly linked to our ability and willingness to share life-affirming practices that come from a unified quantum worldview.

To do justice to the huge concepts implied by *The Divine Matrix,* I've written it in three parts, each covering one of the key implications of the field. Rather than creating a formal conclusion at the end of each part, I've highlighted the important concepts as an in-line summary, noting such an idea as a "Key" designated by number (as in Key 1, Key 2, and so forth). For quick reference, a listing of the 20 Keys may be found at the end of Chapter 8.

A brief description of each section will help in navigating the material and in finding the information that's useful for everything from important references to deep inspiration.

Part I, "Discovering the Divine Matrix: The Mystery That Connects All Things," explores the enduring human sense that we're united by a field of energy that connects everything. In Chapter 1, I describe the single experiment that set scientists back over 100 years in the search for such a unified field. It is in this section that I also share the 20th-century research that led to advances in quantum physics forcing scientists to revisit the original experiment that told us everything is separate. This includes three representative experiments showing the latest scientific documentation of a previously unrecognized field of energy. Briefly, these findings demonstrate the following:

1. Human DNA has a direct effect on the stuff that our world is made of.

2. Human emotion has a direct effect on the DNA that affects the stuff that our world is made of.

3. The relationship between emotions and DNA transcends the bounds of time and space. The effects are the same regardless of distance.

At the end of Part I, there can be little doubt as to the existence of the Divine Matrix. Whether we're describing it from a spiritual or scientific perspective, it's clear that there's something out there—a field of energy that connects everything we do, as well as all that we are and experience. The logical questions then become "What do we do with this information?" and "How do we use the Divine Matrix in our lives?"

Part II, "The Bridge Between Imagination and Reality: How the Divine Matrix Works," explores what it means to live in a universe where in addition to simply being connected (nonlocal), everything is linked *holographically*. The subtle power of these principles is perhaps one of the greatest discoveries of 20th-century physics—and at the same time, it's quite possibly the least understood and most overlooked. This section is intentionally nontechnical and designed to be a useful guide to the mystery of experiences that we all share yet rarely recognize in their fullest capacity to teach us.

When we look at our lives from the viewpoint that everything is everywhere all the time, the implications are so vast that for many they're hard to grasp. It's precisely because of our universal connection that we're empowered to support, share, and participate in life's joys and tragedies anywhere, anytime. How do we make use of such power?

The answer begins with our understanding that there really is no "here" and "there," or "then" and "now." From the perspective of life as a universally connected hologram, *here is already there,* and *then has always been now.* Ancient spiritual traditions remind us that in each moment of the day, we make the choices that either affirm or deny our lives. Every second we choose to nourish ourselves in a way that supports or depletes our lives; to breathe deep and life-affirming breaths or shallow, life-denying ones; and to think and speak about other people in a manner that is honoring or dishonoring.

Through the power of our nonlocal, holographic consciousness, each of these seemingly insignificant choices has consequences that extend well beyond the places and the moments of our lives. Our individual choices combine to become our collective reality—that's what makes the discoveries both exciting and frightening. Through these understandings, we see:

- Why our good wishes, thoughts, and prayers are already at their destination

- That we aren't limited by our bodies or the "laws" of physics

- How we support our loved ones everywhere from the battlefield to the boardroom—without ever leaving our home

- That we *do* have the potential to heal instantaneously

- That it *is* possible to see across time and space without ever opening our eyes

Part III, "Messages from the Divine Matrix: Living, Loving, and Healing in Quantum Awareness," delves directly into the practical aspects of what it means to live in a unified field of energy, along with how it affects the events of our lives. With examples of synchronicities and coincidences, powerful acts of intentional healing, and what our most intimate relationships are showing us, this section serves as a template to recognize what similar experiences may mean in our own lives.

Through a series of real case histories, I share the power, irony, and clarity of how seemingly insignificant events in our lives are actually "us" showing ourselves our truest and deepest beliefs. Among the examples used to describe this relationship, I include a case history of how our pets can show us with *their* bodies the physical conditions that have either gone unnoticed or are still developing in our own.

The Divine Matrix is the result of more than 20 years of research, as well as my personal journey to make sense of the great secret held in our most ancient, mystical, and cherished traditions. If you've always sought to answer the questions "Are we *really* connected, and if so, how deep does that connection go?" and "How much power do we really have to change our world?" then you'll like this book.

The Divine Matrix is written for those of you whose lives bridge the reality of our past with the hope of our future. It is you who are being asked to forgive and find compassion in a world reeling from the scars of hurt, judgment, and fear. The key to surviving our time in history is to create a new way of thinking while we're still living in the conditions that threaten our existence.

Ultimately, we may discover that our ability to understand and apply the "rules" of the Divine Matrix holds the key to our deepest healing, our greatest joy, and our survival as a species.

— **Gregg Braden**
Santa Fe, New Mexico

PART I

DISCOVERING THE
DiViNE MATRiX:
THE MYSTERY THAT
CONNECTS ALL THINGS

CHAPTER ONE

Q: WHAT'S IN THE SPACE BETWEEN?
A: *THE DiViNE MATRiX*

> *"Science cannot solve the ultimate mystery of nature. And that is because, in the last analysis, we ourselves are . . . part of the mystery that we are trying to solve."*
> — Max Planck (1858–1947), physicist

> *"When we understand us, our consciousness, we also understand the universe and the separation disappears."*
> — Amit Goswami, physicist

There is a place where all things begin, a location of pure energy that simply "is." In this quantum incubator for reality, all things are possible. From our personal success, abundance, and healing to our failure, lack, and disease . . . everything from our greatest fear to our deepest desire begins in this "soup" of potential.

Through the reality makers of imagination, expectation, judgment, passion, and prayer, we galvanize each possibility into existence. In our beliefs about who we are, what we have and don't have, and what should and shouldn't be, we breathe life into our greatest joys as well as our darkest moments.

The key to mastering this place of pure energy is to know that it exists, to understand how it works, and finally to speak the language that it recognizes. All things become available to us as the architects of reality in this place where the world begins: the pure space of the Divine Matrix.

Key 1: The Divine Matrix is the *container* that holds the universe, the *bridge* between all things, and the *mirror* that shows us what we have created.

The last thing I expected to see on a late October afternoon hiking in a remote canyon of the Four Corners area in northwestern New Mexico was a Native American wisdom keeper walking toward me on the same trail. Yet there he was, standing at the top of the small incline that separated us as our paths converged that day.

I'm not sure how long he'd been there. By the time I saw him, he was just waiting, watching me as I stepped carefully among the loose stones on the path. The low sun created a glow that cast a deep shadow across the man's body. As I held my hand up to block the light from my eyes, I could see a few locks of shoulder-length hair blowing across his face.

He seemed as surprised to see me as I was to see him. The wind carried the sound of his voice toward me as he cupped his hands on either side of his mouth. "Hello!" he shouted.

"Hello," I called back. "I didn't expect to see anyone here this time of day." Stepping a little closer, I asked, "How long have you been watching me?"

"Not long," he replied. "I come here to listen to the voices of my ancestors in those caves," he said, as one arm pointed toward the other side of the canyon.

The path we were following wound through a series of archaeological sites built nearly 11 centuries before by a mysterious clan of people. No one knows where they came from or who they were. With no evidence of their skills evolving over time, the people that modern natives simply call "the ancient ones" showed up one day in history and brought with them the most advanced technology that would be seen in North America for another thousand years.

From the four-story-tall buildings and perfect stone kivas (round ceremonial structures) buried in the ground to the vast irrigation systems and the sophisticated crops that sustained the people, this place seems to have just appeared one day. And then those who built it were suddenly gone—they just vanished.

The ancient ones left precious few clues to tell us who they were. With the exception of the rock art on the canyon walls, no written records have ever been found. There are no sites of mass burials or cremations, or weapons of war. Yet the evidence of their existence is there: hundreds of ancient dwellings in an 11-mile-long, 1-mile-wide canyon in the remote corner of a desolate canyon in northwestern New Mexico.

I've gone to this place often to walk, immerse myself in the strange beauty of the open desolation, and feel the past. On that late October afternoon, both the wisdom keeper and I had come to the high desert on the same day for the same reason. As we exchanged our beliefs about the secrets still held there, my new friend shared a story.

A LONG TIME AGO . . .

"A long time ago, our world was very different from the way we see it today," the wisdom keeper began. "There were fewer people, and we lived closer to the land. People knew the language of the rain, the crops, and the Great Creator. They even knew how to speak to the stars and the sky people. They were aware that life is sacred and comes from the marriage between Mother Earth and Father Sky. In this time, there was balance and people were happy."

I felt something very ancient well up inside of me as I heard the man's peaceful voice echo against the sandstone cliffs that surrounded us. Suddenly, his voice changed to a tone of sadness.

"Then something happened," he said. "No one really knows why, but people started to forget who they were. In their forgetting, they began to feel separate—separate from the earth, from each other, and even from the one who created them. They were lost and wandered through life with no direction or connection. In their separation, they believed that they had to fight to survive in this world and defend themselves against the same forces that gave them the life they had learned to live in harmony with and trust. Soon all of their energy was used to protect themselves from the world around them, instead of making peace with the world within them."

Immediately, the man's story resonated with me. As I listened to what he was telling me, it sounded as if he were describing human beings today! With the few exceptions of isolated cultures and remote pockets of tradition that remain, our civilization certainly places its focus more on the world *around* us and less on the world *within* us.

We spend hundreds of millions of dollars each year defending ourselves from disease and trying to control nature. In doing so, we have perhaps strayed further from our balance with the natural world than ever before. The wisdom keeper had my attention—now the question was, where was he going with his story?

"Even though they had forgotten who they were, somewhere inside of them the gift of their ancestors remained," he continued. "There was still a memory that lived within them. In their dreams at night they knew that they held the power to heal their bodies, bring rain when they needed to, and speak with their ancestors. They knew that somehow they could find their place in the natural world once again.

"As they tried to remember who they were, they began to build the things *outside* of their bodies that reminded them of who they were on the *inside*. As time went on, they even built machines to do their healing, made chemicals to grow their crops, and stretched wires to communicate over long distances. The farther they wandered from their inner power, the more cluttered their outer lives became with the things that they believed would make them happy."

As I listened, I saw the unmistakable parallels between the people I was hearing about and our civilization today. Our civilization has become steeped in feelings of being powerless to help ourselves or make a better world. So often we feel *helpless* as we watch our loved ones slip away from us into the clutches of pain and addictions. We think that we're *powerless* to ease the suffering from the horrible diseases that no living thing should ever have to endure. We can only *hope* for the peace that will bring those we care about safely from the terror of foreign battlefields. And together, we feel insignificant in the presence of a growing nuclear threat as the world aligns itself along the divisions of religious beliefs, bloodlines, and borders.

It seems that the farther we stray from our natural relationship with the earth, our bodies, one another, and God, the emptier we become. In our emptiness, we strive to fill our inner void with "things." When we look at the world from this perspective, I cannot help but think of a similar dilemma portrayed in the science-fiction movie *Contact*. The President's science advisor (played by Matthew McConaughey) explores the fundamental question that faces every technological society. During a television interview, he asks if we are a better society because of our technology—has it brought us closer together or made us feel more separate? The question is never really answered in the movie, and the topic could fill an entire book unto itself. However, the point that the advisor is making when he asks how much of our power we give away to our diversions is a good one.

When we feel that video games, movies, virtual online relationships, and voiceless communication are necessities and they become substitutes for real life and face-to-face contact, this may be signs of a society in trouble. While electronics and entertainment media certainly seem to make life more interesting, they could also be red flags telling us how far we've strayed from our power to live rich, healthy, and meaningful lives.

Additionally, when the focus of our lives becomes how to *avoid disease* rather than how to live in a healthy way, how to *stay out of war* rather than how to cooperate in peace, and how to *create new weapons* rather than how to live in a world where armed conflict has become obsolete, clearly the path we're on has become one of survival. In such a mode, no one is truly happy—nobody really "wins." When we find ourselves living this way, the obvious thing to do would be to look for another route. And that's precisely what this book is about and why I'm sharing this story.

"How does the story end?" I asked the wisdom keeper. "Did the people ever find their power and remember who they were?"

By this time, the sun had disappeared behind the canyon walls, and for the first time I could actually see who I was talking to. The sun-darkened man standing in front of me smiled broadly upon hearing my question. He was quiet for just a moment, and then he whispered, "No one knows because the story isn't finished. The people who got lost are our ancestors, and we are the ones who are writing the ending. What do you think . . . ?"

I only saw the man a couple of times after that in various places throughout the land and communities that we both love. I think about him often, though. As I see the events of the world unfold, I remember his story and wonder if we'll complete the ending in this lifetime. Will you and I be the ones who remember?

The implications of the story that the man in the canyon shared are vast. The conventional wisdom of history is that the tools of past civilizations—no matter how ancient—were somehow less advanced than modern technology. While it's true that these peoples might not have used "modern" science to solve their problems, they may have had something even better.

In discussions with historians and archaeologists whose livelihoods are based on interpreting the past, this topic is generally the source of passionately heated emotion. "If they were so advanced, where's the evidence of their technology?" the experts ask. "Where are their toasters, microwave ovens, and VCRs?" I find it very interesting that in interpreting the development of a civilization, so much could hinge on the *things* that the individuals built. What about the thinking that underlies what they made? While to the best of my knowledge, it's true that we've never found a TV or digital camera in the archaeological record of the American Southwest (or anywhere else for that matter), the question is why?

Is it possible that when we see the remains of advanced civilizations, such as those in Egypt, Peru, or the American Desert Southwest, we're actually witnessing the remnants of a technology *so advanced* that they didn't need toasters and VCRs? Maybe they outgrew the need for a cluttered and complex outer world. Perhaps they knew something about themselves that gave them the *inner technology* to live in a different way, knowledge that we've forgotten. That wisdom could have given them everything that they needed to sustain their lives and heal in a way that we're only beginning to understand.

If this is true, then perhaps we need look no further than nature to understand who we are and what our role in life really is. And maybe some of our most profound and empowering insights are already available in the mysterious discoveries of the quantum world. During the last century, physicists discovered that the stuff that makes up our bodies and our universe doesn't always follow the neat and tidy laws of physics that have been held sacred for nearly three centuries. In fact, on the tiniest scales of our world, the very particles that we're made of break the rules that say we're separate from one another and limited in our existence. On the particle level, everything appears to be connected and infinite.

These discoveries suggest that there's something within each of us that isn't limited by time, space, or even death. The bottom line of these findings is that we appear to live in a "nonlocal" universe where everything is always connected.

Dean Radin, senior scientist for the Institute of Noetic Sciences, has been a pioneer in exploring just what it means for us to live in such a world. "Nonlocality," he explains, "means that there are ways in which things that appear to be separate are, in fact, not separate."[1] There are aspects of us, Radin suggests, that extend beyond the here-and-now and allow us to be spread throughout space and time. In other words, the "us" that lives in our physical selves isn't limited by the skin and hair that define our bodies.

Whatever we choose to call that mysterious "something," we all have it; and ours mingles with everyone else's as part of the field of energy that bathes all things. This field is believed to be the quantum net that connects the universe, as well as the infinitely microscopic and energetic blueprint for everything from healing our bodies to forging world peace. To recognize our true power, we must understand what this field is and how it works.

If the ancient ones in that northern New Mexican canyon—or anywhere else in the world, for that matter—understood how this forgotten part of us works, then it makes tremendous sense for us to honor the knowledge of our ancestors and find a place for their wisdom in our time.

ARE WE CONNECTED—<u>REALLY</u> CONNECTED?

Modern science is hot on the trail of solving one of the greatest mysteries of all time. You may not hear about it during the evening news, and you probably won't see it on the front page of *USA Today* or *The Wall Street Journal*. Yet nearly 70 years of research in an area of science known as the "new physics" is pointing to a conclusion that we can't escape.

Key 2: Everything in our world is connected to everything else.

That's it—really! That's the news that changes everything and is absolutely shaking the foundations of science as we know it today.

"Okay," you say, "we've heard this before. What makes *this* conclusion so different? What does it really mean to be so connected?" These are very good questions, and the answers may surprise you. The difference between the new discoveries and what we previously believed is that in the past we were simply *told* that the connection exists. Through technical phrases such as "sensitive dependence on initial conditions" (or "the butterfly effect") and theories suggesting that what we do "here" has an effect "there," we could vaguely observe the connection playing out in our lives. The new experiments, however, take us one step beyond.

In addition to proving that we're linked to everything, research now demonstrates that the connection exists *because* of us. Our connectedness gives us the power to stack the deck in our favor when it comes to the way our lives turn out. In everything from searching for romance and healing our loved ones to the fulfillment of our deepest aspirations, we are an integral part of all that we experience each day.

The fact that the discoveries show that we can use our connection consciously opens the door to nothing less than our opportunity to tap the same power that drives the entire universe. Through the oneness that lives inside of you, me, and all humans who walk the planet, we have a direct line to the same force that creates everything from atoms and stars to the DNA of life!

There's one small catch, however: Our power to do so is dormant until we awaken it. The key to awakening such an awesome power is to make a small shift in the way we see ourselves in the world. Just as Logue's initiates found that they could fly after receiving a little nudge off the cliff (from the poem on page ix), with a small shift in perception we can tap the most powerful force in the universe in order to address even seemingly impossible situations. This happens when we allow ourselves a new way of seeing our role in the world.

Because the universe seems like a really big place—almost too vast for us to even think about—we can begin by seeing ourselves differently in our everyday lives. The "small shift" that we need is to see ourselves as *part of* the world rather than *separate from* it. The way to convince ourselves that we're truly one with everything that we see and experience is to understand *how* we're joined and *what* that connection means.

Key 3: To tap the force of the universe itself, we must see ourselves as *part of* the world rather than *separate from* it.

Through the connection that joins all things, the "stuff" that the universe is made of (waves and particles of energy) appears to break the laws of time and space as we once knew them. Although the details sound like science fiction, they're very real. Particles of light (photons), for example, have been observed to bilocate—that is, to be in two different places separated by many miles at precisely the same instant.

From the DNA of our bodies to the atoms of everything else, things in nature appear to share information more rapidly than Albert Einstein predicted anything could ever travel—faster than the speed of light. In some experiments, data has even arrived at its destination *before* it's left its place of origin! Historically, such phenomena were believed to be impossible, but apparently they're not only possible, they also may be showing us something more than just the interesting anomalies of small units of matter. The freedom of movement that the quantum particles demonstrate may reveal how the rest of the universe works when we look beyond what we know of physics.

While these results may sound like the futuristic script of a *Star Trek* episode, they're being observed now, under the scrutiny of present-day scientists. Individually, the experiments that produce such effects are certainly fascinating and deserve more investigation. Considered together, however, they also suggest that we may not be as limited by the laws of physics as we believe. Perhaps things *are* able to travel faster than the speed of light, and maybe they *can* be in two places at once! And if *things* have this ability, what about us?

These are precisely the possibilities that excite today's innovators and stir our own imaginations. It is in the coupling of the imagination—the idea of something that could be—with an emotion that gives life to a possibility that it becomes a reality. Manifestation begins with the willingness to make room in our beliefs for something that supposedly doesn't exist. We create that "something" through the force of consciousness and awareness.

The poet William Blake recognized the power of imagination as the essence of our existence, rather than something that we simply experience occasionally in our spare time. "Man is all imagination," he said, clarifying, "The Eternal Body of Man is the Imagination, that is, God Himself."[2] Philosopher and poet John Mackenzie further explained our relationship with the imagination, suggesting, "The distinction between what is real and what is imaginary is not one that can be finely maintained . . . all existing things are . . . imaginary."[3] In both these descriptions, the concrete events of life must first be envisioned as possibilities before they can become a reality.

However, for the imaginary ideas of one moment in time to become the reality of another, there must be something that links them together. Somehow in the fabric of the universe there must be a connection between past imaginings and present and future realities. Einstein firmly believed that the past and the future are intimately entwined as the stuff of the fourth dimension, a reality that he called *space-time*. "The distinction between past, present, and future," he said, "is only a stubbornly persistent illusion."[4]

So, in ways that we are only beginning to understand, we find that we're connected not only with everything that we see in our lives today, but also with everything that's ever been, as well as with things that haven't happened yet. And what we're experiencing *now* is the outcome of events that have occurred (at least in part) in a realm of the universe that we can't even see.

The implications of these relationships are huge. In a world where an intelligent field of energy connects everything from global peace to personal healing, what may have sounded like fantasy and miracles in the past suddenly becomes possible in our lives.

With these connections in mind, we must begin to think of the way that we relate to life, our families, and even our casual acquaintances from a powerful new perspective. Good or bad, right or wrong, everything from the lightest and most beautiful life experiences to the most horrible occasions of human suffering can no longer be written off as chance happenings. Clearly, the key to healing; peace; abundance; and the creation of experiences, careers, and relationships that bring us joy is to understand just how deeply we're connected to everything in our reality.

SEARCHING FOR THE MATRIX

I remember the first time I relayed the news of our connectedness to my Native American friend from the canyon. During an unexpected meeting in a local market, I passionately shared information from a press release I'd just read about a "new" field of energy that had been discovered, a unifying field unlike any other energy known to exist.

"It's this field of energy," I blurted out, "that connects everything. It connects us with the world, one another, and even with the universe beyond Earth, just like you and I have talked about in the past."

In a way that was typical of my friend, he was quiet for a moment as he honored my excitement. After a few seconds, he took a breath and then replied with a directness that I'd seen many times before.

He was honest and to the point. "So!" he said. "You have found that everything is connected. That is what our people have been saying all along. It is good that your science has figured it out, too!"

If an intelligent field of energy really plays such a powerful role in how the universe works, then why didn't we know about it until recently? We've just emerged from the 20th century, a time historians may well come to regard as the most remarkable period in history. Within a single generation, we learned how to unleash the power of the atom, to store a library the size of a city block on a computer chip, and to read and engineer the DNA of life. How could we have accomplished all of these scientific marvels yet missed the single most important discovery of all, the one understanding that gives us access to the power of creation itself? The answer may surprise you.

There was a time in our not-so-distant past when scientists did, in fact, attempt to solve the mystery of whether or not we're connected through an intelligent field of energy by proving once and for all whether or not the field even exists. While the idea of the investigation was good, more than 100 years later we're still recovering from the way in which this famous experiment was interpreted. As a result, for most of the 20th century, if scientists dared to mention anything about a unifying field of energy that connects everything through what is otherwise empty space, they would be laughed out of the classroom or right off the university stage. With few exceptions, the idea wasn't one that was accepted, or even allowed, in serious scientific discussions. However, this hadn't always been the case.

Although our sense of precisely what it is that connects the universe has remained a mystery, there have been countless attempts to name it in order to acknowledge its existence. In the Buddhist Sutras, for example, the realm of the great god Indra is described as the place where the web that connects the entire universe originates: "Far away in the heavenly abode of the great god Indra, there is a wonderful net which has been hung by some cunning artificer in such a manner that it stretches out infinitely in all directions."[5]

In the Hopi creation story, it is said that the current cycle of our world began long ago when Spider Grandmother emerged into the emptiness of this world. The first thing she did was to spin the great web that connects all things, and through it she created the place where her children would live their lives.

Since the time of the ancient Greeks, those who believed in a universal field of energy that connects everything have simply referred to it as the *ether*. In Greek mythology, ether was thought of as the essence of space itself and described as the "air breathed by the gods." Both Pythagoras and Aristotle identified it as the mysterious fifth element of creation, following the four familiar elements of fire, air, water, and earth. In later times, alchemists continued to use the words of the Greeks to describe our world— terminology that endured until the birth of modern science.

Contradicting the traditional views of most scientists today, some of the greatest minds in history have not only believed that ether exists; many of them even took its existence one step further. They said that ether is *necessary* for the laws of physics to work as they do. During the 1600s, Sir Isaac Newton, the "father" of modern science, used the word *ether* to describe an invisible substance that permeates the entire universe, which he believed was responsible for gravity as well as the sensations of the body. He thought of it as a living spirit, although he recognized that the equipment to validate its existence wasn't available in his day.

It wasn't until the 19th century that the man who proposed electromagnetic theory, James Clerk Maxwell, formally offered a scientific description of the ether that connects all things. He described it as a "material substance of a more subtle kind than visible bodies, supposed to exist in those parts of space which are apparently empty."[6]

As recently as the early 20th century, some of the most respected scientific minds still used the ancient terminology to describe the essence that fills empty space. They thought of the ether as an actual substance with a consistency that was somewhere between physical matter and pure energy. It is through the ether, the scientists reasoned, that light waves can move from one point to another in what otherwise looks like empty space.

"I cannot but regard the ether, which can be the seat of an electromagnetic field with its energy and its vibrations, as endowed with a certain degree of substantiality, however different it may be from all ordinary matter" stated Nobel Prize–winning physicist Hendrik Lorentz in 1906.[7] Lorentz's equations were the ones that eventually gave Einstein the tools to develop his revolutionary theory of relativity.

Even after his theories seemed to discount the need for ether in the universe, Einstein himself believed that something would be discovered to explain what occupies the emptiness of space, stating, "Space without ether is unthinkable." Similar to the way Lorentz and the ancient Greeks thought of this substance as the conduit through which waves move, Einstein stated that ether is necessary for the laws of physics to exist: "In such space [without ether] there not only would be no propagation of light, but also no possibility of existence for standards of space and time."[8]

Although on the one hand, Einstein appears to acknowledge the possibility of ether, on the other, he cautioned that it shouldn't be thought of as energy in the ordinary sense. "Ether may not be thought of as endowed with the quality characteristic of ponderable media, as consisting of parts ['particles'] which may be tracked through time."[9] In this way he described how, due to ether's unconventional nature, its existence was still compatible with his own theories.

The mere mention of the ether field today still ignites debate about whether or not it exists. Almost in the same breath, it resurrects the memory of one famous experiment that was designed to prove or disprove the field's existence once and for all. As is often the case with this kind of investigation, the outcome raised more questions—and controversy—than it resolved.

HISTORY'S GREATEST "FAILED" EXPERIMENT

Performed more than 100 years ago, the ether experiment is named after the two scientists who designed it, Albert Michelson and Edward Morley. The sole purpose of the Michelson-Morley experiment was to determine whether or not the mysterious ether of the universe did in fact exist. The long-anticipated experiment—devised to verify the results of a similar one performed in 1881—was the buzz of the scientific community that gathered in the laboratory at what is now Case Western Reserve University in 1887.[10] Ultimately, it held consequences that even the best minds of the late 19th century couldn't have known.

The thinking behind the experiment was innovative, to be sure. If ether really exists, Michelson and Morley reasoned, then it must be an energy that is everywhere, quiet, and still. And if this is true, then the earth's passage through this field in space should create a movement that can be measured. Just as we're able to detect the air as it ripples through the vast fields of golden wheat on the plains of Kansas, we should be able to detect the ether's "breeze." Michelson and Morley named this hypothetical phenomenon the *ether wind*.

The pilot of any plane will agree that when an aircraft is flying *with* the currents of the atmosphere, the time to get from one place to another can be much shorter. However, when the plane is flying *against* the flow, it endures a rough ride, and wind resistance can add hours to the flight. Michelson and Morley reasoned that if they could shoot a ray of light in two directions simultaneously, the difference in the amount of time it took for each beam to reach its destination should allow the experimenters to detect the presence and flow of the ether wind. While the experiment was a good idea, the results surprised everyone.

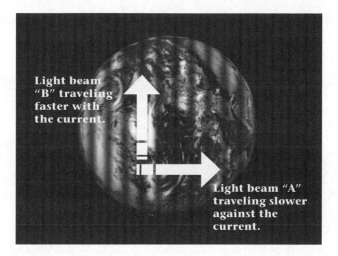

Figure 1. If ether was present, Michelson and Morley believed that a beam of light should travel slower as it moved against the ether's currents (A), and faster as it traveled with the currents (B). The experiment, conducted in 1887, found no ether currents; the conclusion was that no ether exists. The consequences of this interpretation have haunted scientists for more than 100 years. In 1986, the journal *Nature* reported on the results of experiments conducted with more sensitive equipment. The bottom line: A field with the characteristics of the ether was detected, and it behaved just as the older predictions had suggested it would a century before.

The bottom line was that Michelson and Morley's equipment detected no ether wind. Finding what looked like the absence of the wind, both the 1881 and 1887 experiments seemed to lead to the same conclusion: No ether exists. Michelson interpreted the results of what has been called "the most successful failed experiment" in history in the prestigious *American Journal of Science:* "The result of the hypothesis of a stationary ether field is thus shown to be incorrect, and the necessary conclusion follows that the hypothesis is erroneous."[11]

While the experiment may be described as a "failure" with regard to proving the existence of ether, it actually demonstrated that the ether field just might not behave in the way scientists originally expected. Just because no movement was detected doesn't mean that ether wasn't there. An analogy for this would be to hold your finger above your head to test for wind: To conclude that no air existed because you felt no breeze during the test would be a rough equivalent of the thinking behind the conclusions of the 1887 experiment.

Accepting this experiment as proof that ether doesn't exist, modern scientists operate under the assumption that things in our universe happen independently of each other. They accept that what an individual does in one part of the world is completely unrelated to other areas and has no effect on someone else half a planet away. Arguably, this experiment has become the basis for a worldview that has had a profound impact on our lives and the earth. As a consequence of this kind of thinking, we govern our nations, power our cities, test our atomic bombs, and exhaust our resources, believing that what we're doing in one place has no impact anywhere else. Since 1887, we've based the development of an entire civilization on the belief that everything is separate from everything else, a premise that more recent experiments show is simply not true!

Today, more than 100 years after the original experiment, new studies suggest that the ether, or something like it, does in fact exist—it just does not appear to come in the form that Michelson and Morley had expected. Believing that the field must be motionless and made of electricity and magnetism, just as the other forms of energy discovered in the mid-1800s were, they searched for the ether as they would a conventional form of energy. But ether is far from conventional.

In 1986, *Nature* published an unassuming report simply titled "Special Relativity."[12] With implications that absolutely shake the foundation of the Michelson-Morley experiment as well as everything we believe about our connection to the world, it described an experiment by a scientist named E. W. Silvertooth that was sponsored by the U.S. Air Force. Duplicating the 1887 experiment—but with equipment that was much more sensitive— Silvertooth reported that he *did* detect a movement in the ether field. Furthermore, it was precisely linked to the motion of the earth through space, just as had been predicted! This experiment, and others since then, suggest that the ether does in fact exist, just as Planck suggested in 1944.

Although modern experiments continue to indicate that the field is there, we can be sure that it will never be called "ether" again. In scientific circles, the mere mention of the word conjures up adjectives ranging from "pseudoscience" to "hogwash"! As we'll see in Chapter 2, the existence of a universal field of energy that permeates our world is being thought of in very different terms—the experiments that prove its existence are so new that a single name has yet to be chosen. Regardless of what we choose to call it, however, something is definitely there. It connects everything in our world and beyond and affects us in ways that we're only beginning to understand.

So how could this have happened? How might we have missed such a powerful key to understanding how the universe works? The answer to this question cuts to the very core of the quest that's created the most intense controversy and heated debate among the greatest minds of the last two centuries—a dispute that continues to this day. It's all about the way we see ourselves in the world and our interpretation of that viewpoint.

The key is that the energy connecting everything in the universe is also part of what it connects! Rather than thinking of the field as separate from everyday reality, the experiments tell us that the mundane visible world actually originates as the field: It's as if the blanket of the Divine Matrix is spread smoothly throughout the universe, and every once in a while it "wrinkles" here and there into a rock, tree, planet, or person that we recognize. Ultimately, all of these things are just ripples in the field, and this subtle yet powerful shift in thinking is the key to tapping the power of the Divine Matrix in our lives. To do so, however, we must understand why scientists view the world as they do today.

A BRIEF HISTORY OF PHYSICS:
DIFFERENT RULES FOR DIFFERENT WORLDS

Science is simply a language to describe the natural world, along with our relationship to it and the universe beyond. And it is only one language; there have been others (such as *alchemy* and *spirituality,* for example) that were used long before modern science ever came along. While they may not have been sophisticated, they certainly worked. I'm always amazed when people ask, "What did we do before science? Did we know anything about our world?" The answer is a resounding "Yes!" We knew a lot about the universe.

What we knew worked so well that it provided an entire framework for understanding everything from the origins of life, to why we become sick and what to do about it, to how we calculate the cycles of the sun, moon, and stars. While this kind of knowing was obviously not described in the technical language that we're accustomed to today, it did a pretty good job of providing a useful story of how things work and why they are as they are—so good, in fact, that civilization existed for more than 5,000 years without relying upon science as we know it today.

Science and the scientific era are generally acknowledged as beginning in the 1600s. It was in July of 1687 that Isaac Newton formalized the mathematics that seem to describe our everyday world, publishing his classic work *Philosophiae Naturalis Principia Mathematica* (Mathematic Principles of Natural Philosophy).

For more than 200 years, Newton's observations about nature were the foundation of the scientific field now called "classical physics." Along with Maxwell's theories of electricity and magnetism from the late 1800s and Einstein's theories of relativity from the early 1900s, classical physics has been tremendously successful in explaining the large-scale things that we see, such as the movement of planets and apples falling from trees. It has served us so well that we were able to calculate the orbits for our satellites and even put a man on the moon.

During the early 20th century, however, advances in science revealed a place in nature where Newton's laws just don't seem to work: the very small world of the atom. Before then, we simply didn't have the technology to peer into the subatomic world or watch the way particles behave during the birth of a star in a distant galaxy. In both realms—the smallest and the largest—scientists began to see things that couldn't be explained by traditional physics. A new kind of physics had to be developed, with the rules that would explain the exceptions to our everyday world: the things that happen in the realm of quantum physics.

The definition of quantum physics is found in its name. *Quantum* means "a discrete quantity of electromagnetic energy"— thus, it's the stuff that our world is made of when we reduce it to its essence. Quantum physicists soon found that what looks like the solid world to us is really not so solid at all. The following analogy may help us understand why.

When the local movie theater projects a moving image on the screen in front of us, we know that the story we're seeing is an illusion. The romance and tragedy that tug at our heartstrings are actually the result of many still pictures being flashed very quickly, one after another, to create the *sense* of a continuous story. While our eyes do see the single images frame by frame, our brain merges them into what we perceive as nonstop movement.

Quantum physicists believe that our world works in much the same way. For instance, what we see as the football touchdown or figure skater's triple axel on a Sunday-afternoon sports program is actually, in quantum terms, a series of individual events that happen very quickly and closely together. Similar to the way that many images strung together make a movie look so real, life actually occurs as brief, tiny bursts of light called "quanta." The quanta of life happen so quickly that unless our brain is trained to operate differently (as in some forms of meditation), it simply averages the pulses to create the uninterrupted action we see as the Sunday sports.

Quantum physics, then, is the study of the things that happen on the very small scale of the forces that underlie our physical world. The difference in the ways that the quantum and everyday worlds seem to work has created two schools of thought among scientists in contemporary physics: the classical and the quantum. And each has its own theories to support it.

The great challenge has been to marry these two very different kinds of thinking into a single view of the universe—a unified theory. To do so requires the existence of something that fills what we think of as empty space. But what could occupy it?

A SUMMARY OF THE LONG ROAD TO A UNIFIED THEORY

1687—**Newtonian Physics:** Isaac Newton publishes his laws of motion, and modern science begins. This view sees the universe as a massive mechanical system where space and time are absolute.

1867—**Field-Theory Physics:** James Clerk Maxwell proposes the existence of forces that cannot be explained by Newton's physics. His research, along with that of Michael Faraday, leads to the discovery of the universe as fields of energy that interact with each other.

1900—**Quantum Physics:** Max Planck publishes his theory of the world as bursts of energy called "quanta." Experiments on the quantum level show that matter exists as probabilities and tendencies rather than absolute things, suggesting that "reality" may not be so real or solid after all.

1905—**Relativity Physics:** Albert Einstein's view of the universe upsets Newtonian physics. He proposes that time is relative rather than absolute. A key aspect of relativity is that time and space cannot be separated and exist together as a fourth dimension.

1970—**String-Theory Physics:** Physicists discover that theories describing the universe as tiny vibrating strings of energy can be used to explain the observations of both the quantum and everyday worlds. The theory is formally accepted by the mainstream physics community in 1984 as a possible bridge to unite all other theories.

20??—**The New and Improved Unified Theory of Physics:** Someday in the future, physicists will discover a way to explain the holographic nature of what we observe in the quantum universe, as well as what we see in our everyday world. They will formulate the equations to unify their explanation into one consistent story.

WHAT'S IN THE SPACE BETWEEN?

Early in the movie *Contact,* the main character, Dr. Arroway (played by Jodie Foster), asks her father the question that becomes the tagline for the rest of the movie: *Are we alone in the universe?* Her father's answer becomes the touchstone for the things that are true in her life. When she finds herself in particularly vulnerable situations, such as opening herself up to romance or trusting her experience in the distant universe where she's been transported, her father's words become the guiding principle of her beliefs: His response is simply that if we're alone in the universe, it seems like an awful waste of space.

In much the same way, if we believe that the space between any two things is empty, then it seems like a tremendous waste as well. Scientists believe that more than 90 percent of the cosmos is "missing" and appears to us as empty space. That means that of the entire universe as we know it, only 10 percent has anything in it. Do you really believe that the 10 percent of creation we occupy is all there is? What's in the space that we think of as "empty"?

If it's really vacant, then there's a big question that must be answered: How can the waves of energy that transmit everything from our cell-phone calls to the reflected light bringing this page's words to your eyes travel from one place to another? Just as water carries ripples away from the place where a stone is tossed into a pond, something must exist that conveys the vibrations of life from one point to another. For this to be true, however, we must upset one of the key tenets of modern science: the belief that space is empty.

When we can at last resolve the mystery of what the space is made of, we will have taken a great step toward understanding ourselves and our relation to the world around us. This question, as we shall see, is as old as we humans are. And the answer, we'll also discover, has probably been with us all along.

Our sense that we're somehow connected to the universe, our world, and one another has been a constant, from the aboriginal history etched into the cliff walls of Australia (now believed to be more than 20,000 years old) to the temples of ancient Egypt and the rock art of the American Southwest. While that belief appears to be stronger than ever today, precisely what it is that joins us continues to be the subject of controversy and debate. For us to be connected, there must be something that does the connecting. From poets and philosophers to scientists and those who seek their answers beyond the accepted ideas of their day, humanity has had a sense that within the emptiness we call "space," something is actually there.

Physicist Konrad Finagle (1858–1936) posed the obvious question regarding the significance of space itself, asking, "Consider what would happen if you took away the space from between matter. Everything in the universe would scrunch together into a volume no larger than a dust speck. . . . Space is what keeps everything from happening in the same place."[13] The pioneering anthropologist Louis Leakey once stated, "Without an understanding of who we are, we cannot truly advance." I believe that there is a lot of truth to this statement. The way we've seen ourselves in the past worked well enough to get us where we are today. Now it's time to open the door to a new view of ourselves, one that allows for an even greater possibility. It may be that our reluctance to accept just what it means for space to be occupied by an intelligent force, and for us to be part of that space, has been the biggest stumbling block in our understanding of who we are and how the universe really works.

In the 20th century, modern science may have discovered what's inside of empty space: a field of energy that's different from any other form of energy. Just as Indra's web and Newton's ether suggest, this energy appears to be everywhere, always, and to have existed since the very beginning of time. In a 1928 lecture, Albert Einstein said, "According to the general theory of relativity, space without ether is unthinkable; for in such space there not only would be no propagation of light, but also no possibility of existence for standards of space."[14]

Max Planck stated that the existence of the field suggests that intelligence is responsible for our physical world. "We must assume behind this force [that we see as matter] the existence of a *conscious and intelligent Mind*." He concluded, "This Mind is the *matrix* of all matter [author's brackets and italics]."[15]

THE TAIL OF EINSTEIN'S LION

Whether we talk about the cosmic gap between distant stars and galaxies or the microspace between the bands of energy that form an atom, we ordinarily perceive the space between things as empty. When we say that something is "empty," we typically mean that nothing—absolutely nothing at all—exists there.

Without a doubt, to the untrained eye what we call "space" certainly looks vacant. But how empty can it be? When we really think about it, what would it mean to live in a world where the space between matter is truly void of anything? First, we know that to find such a place in the cosmos is probably impossible for one reason: As the saying goes, nature abhors a vacuum. If we could somehow magically transport ourselves to such a location, however, what would life look like?

To begin with, it would be a very dark place. While we could turn a flashlight "on," for example, its illumination couldn't travel anywhere because there would be nothing for the light waves to pass through. It would be as if we'd thrown a stone into a dried-up pond and were looking for ripples on the surface. The rock would hit the bottom, whether or not the water was there, but there would be no waves, as the ripples that would normally radiate from the impact would have no medium to move through.

For precisely the same reason, our hypothetical world would also be very quiet. Sound must also travel through some kind of medium to perpetuate itself. In fact, almost any kind of energy as we know it today—from the motion of wind to the heat of the sun—couldn't exist because the electrical, magnetic, and radiant fields—and even the fields of gravity—wouldn't have the same meaning in a world where space was truly devoid of anything.

Fortunately, we don't have to speculate about what such a world would be like, since the space that surrounds us is anything but empty. Regardless of what we call it or how science and religion define it, it's clear that there's a field or presence that is the "great net" that connects everything in creation and links us to the higher power of a greater world.

Early in the 20th century, Einstein made reference to the mysterious force that he was certain exists in what we see as the universe around us. "Nature shows us only the tail of the lion," he stated, suggesting that there's something more to what we see as reality, even if we can't see it from our particular cosmic vantage point. With a beauty and eloquence that's typical of Einstein's view of the universe, he elaborated on his analogy of the cosmos: "I do not doubt that the lion belongs to it [the tail] even though he cannot at once reveal himself because of his enormous size."[16] In later writings, Einstein went on to say that regardless of who we are or what our role in the universe may be, we're all subject to a greater power: "Human beings, vegetables, or cosmic dust—we all dance to a mysterious tune, intoned in the distance by an invisible piper."[17]

With his declaration of an intelligence underlying creation, Planck had described the energy of Einstein's lion. By doing so, he ignited a flame of controversy that continues to burn more intensely than ever today. At the center of it, the old ideas about what our world is made of (and the reality of the universe, for that matter) have flown right out the window! More than half a century ago, the father of quantum theory told us that everything is connected through a very real, although unconventional, energy.

CONNECTED AT THE SOURCE: QUANTUM ENTANGLEMENT

Since Planck offered his equations of quantum physics early in the 20th century, many theories have developed and numerous experiments have been performed that seem to precisely prove that notion.

On the smallest levels of the universe, atoms and subatomic particles do in fact act as if they're connected. The problem is that scientists don't know how or even if the behavior that's observed on such tiny scales has any meaning for the larger realities of our daily lives. If it does, then the findings suggest that the amazing technologies of science fiction may soon be the reality of our world!

As recently as 2004, physicists from Germany, China, and Austria published reports that sounded more like fantasy than a scientific experiment. In *Nature,* the scientists announced the first documented experiments of open-destination teleportation—that is, sending the quantum information about a particle (its energetic blueprint) to different locations at the same time.[18] In other words, the process is like "faxing a document and in the process destroying the original."[19]

Other experiments have demonstrated equally impossible-sounding feats, such as "beaming" particles from one place to another and bilocating. As different as each investigation sounds from the others, they all share a common denominator that implies an even greater story. For these experiments to work as they do, a medium must exist—in other words, there has to be something for the particles to move through. And herein lies what may be the greatest mystery of modern times, since conventional physics states that this medium doesn't exist.

In 1997, scientific journals throughout the world published the results of something that traditional physicists say shouldn't have happened. Reported to over 3,400 journalists, educators, scientists, and engineers in more than 40 countries, an experiment had been performed by the University of Geneva in Switzerland on the stuff that our world is made of—particles of light called *photons*—with results that continue to shake the foundation of conventional wisdom.[20]

Specifically, the scientists had split a single photon into two separate particles, creating "twins" with identical properties. Then, using equipment developed for the experiment, they fired both particles away from one another in opposite directions. The twins were placed in a specially designed chamber with two fiber-optic pathways, just like the ones that transmit phone calls, extending away from the chamber in opposite directions for a distance of seven miles. By the time each twin reached its target, 14 miles separated one from the other. At the end of the pathway, the twins were forced to "choose" between two random routes that were identical in every respect.

What makes this experiment so interesting is that when the twin particles reached the place where they had to follow one course or the other, they both made precisely the same choices and traveled the same path each time. Without fail, the results were identical every time the experiment was conducted.

Even though conventional wisdom states that the twins are separate and have no communication with one another, they *act* as if they're still connected! Physicists call this mysterious connection "quantum entanglement." The project leader, Nicholas Gisin, explains, "What is fascinating is that entangled photons form one and the same object. Even when the twin photons are separated geographically, if one of them is modified, the other photon automatically undergoes the same change."[21]

Historically, there's been absolutely nothing in traditional physics that would account for what the experiments showed. Yet we see it time and again in experiments such as Gisin's. Dr.

Raymond Chiao of the University of California at Berkeley further describes the results of the Geneva experiments as "one of the deep mysteries of quantum mechanics. These connections are a fact of nature proven by experiments, but to try to explain them philosophically is very difficult."[22]

The reason why these investigations are important to us is that conventional wisdom would have us believe that there's no way for the photons to communicate with one another—their choices are independent and not related. Our belief has been that when physical objects in this world are separate, they are really *separate* in every sense of the word. But the photons are showing us something very different.

Commenting on this kind of phenomenon long before the 1997 experiment actually took place, Albert Einstein called the possibility of such results occurring "spooky action at a distance." Today scientists believe that these unconventional results are properties that occur only in the quantum realm and acknowledge them as "quantum weirdness."

The connection between the photons was so complete that it appeared to be instantaneous. Once it was recognized on the very small scale of photons, the same phenomenon was subsequently found to exist in other places in nature, even in galaxies separated by light-years of distance. "In principle, it should make no difference whether the correlation between twin particles occurs when they are separated by a few meters or by the entire universe," says Gisin. Why? What connects two particles of light or two galaxies to such a degree that a change in the first happens simultaneously in the second? What are we being shown about the way the world works that we may have missed in earlier experiments from the past?

To answer this kind of question, we first have to understand where the Divine Matrix comes from. And to do that, we have to take a step back—way back—to the time that Western scientists believe is the beginning of everything . . . or at least of the universe as we know it.

THE ORIGIN OF THE MATRIX

Mainstream scientists today believe that our universe began between 13 and 20 billion years ago with a massive explosion unlike anything that had ever existed before or has existed since. Although there are conflicting theories about the precise timing and whether there were single or multiple explosions, there appears to be a general agreement that our universe began with a massive release of energy a long time ago. In 1951, astronomer Fred Hoyle coined a term for that unfathomable explosion that is still used today: He named it the "big bang."

Researchers have calculated that just fractions of a second before the big bang occurred, our entire universe was much, much smaller than it is today. Computer models suggest that it was so small, in fact, that it was tightly compressed into one tiny ball. With all the "empty" space removed from what we see as the universe today, that ball is believed to have been about the size of a single green pea!

While it may have been tiny, it certainly wasn't cool, however. The models suggest that the temperature within that compact space was an unimaginable 18 billion million million million degrees Fahrenheit—many times hotter than the present temperature of the sun. Within a fraction of a second following the big bang, the simulations show that the temperatures may have cooled to a balmy 18 billion degrees or so, and the birth of our new universe was well under way.

As the big bang's explosive force ripped into the emptiness of the existing void, it carried with it more than just the heat and light that we'd expect. It also burst forth as a pattern of energy that became the blueprint for all that is now and all that can ever be. It's this pattern that's the subject of ancient myth, timeless lore, and mystical wisdom. With names that range from the Buddhist Sutra's "net" of Indra, to the Hopi tradition's "web" of Spider Grandmother, the echo of that pattern remains today.

It is this net or web of energy that continues to expand throughout the cosmos as the quantum essence of all things, including us and our surroundings. This is the energy that connects our lives as the Divine Matrix. It is this essence as well that acts as a many-dimensional mirror, reflecting what we create in our emotions and beliefs back to us as our world. (See Part III.)

How can we be so sure that *everything* in the universe is really connected? To answer this question, let's go back to the big bang and the University of Geneva experiment in the previous section. As different as they appear from one another, there's a subtle similarity: In each, the connection that's being explored exists between two things that were once physically joined. In the case of the experiment, splitting a single photon into two identical particles created the twins, and this was done to assure that both were alike in every way. The fact that the photons and the particles from the big bang were once physically part of one another is the key to their connectivity. It appears that once something is joined, *it is always connected,* whether it remains physically linked or not.

> **Key 4:** Once something is joined, *it is always connected,* whether it remains physically linked or not.

This is key in our discussion for one really important and often-overlooked reason. As huge as our universe looks to us today, and notwithstanding the billions of light-years that it takes for the brilliance of the most distant stars to reach our eyes, at one time all the matter in the universe was squeezed into a very small space. In that unimaginable state of compression, everything was physically joined. As the energy of the big bang caused our universe to expand, the matter's particles became separated by greater and greater amounts of space.

The experiments suggest that regardless of how much space separates two things, once joined they are always connected. There's every reason to believe that the entangled state that links particles that are separated today also applies to the stuff of our universe that was connected before the big bang. Technically, everything that was merged within our pea-sized cosmos 13 to 20 billion years ago is still connected! And the energy that does the connecting is what Planck described as the "matrix" of everything.

Today, modern science has refined our understanding of Planck's matrix, describing it as a form of energy that's been everywhere, always present since time began with the big bang. The existence of this field implies three principles that have a direct effect upon the way we live, all that we do, what we believe, and even how we feel about each day of our lives. Admittedly, these ideas directly contradict many well-established beliefs of both science and spirituality. At the same time, though, it is precisely these principles that open the door to an empowering and life-affirming way of seeing our world and living our lives:

1. The first principle suggests that because everything exists *within* the Divine Matrix, all things are connected. If this is so, then what we do in one part of our lives must have an effect and influence on other parts.

2. The second principle proposes that the Divine Matrix is *holographic*—meaning that any portion of the field contains everything in the field. As consciousness itself is believed to be holographic, this signifies that the prayer we make in our living room, for example, *already exists* with our loved ones and at the place where it's intended. In other words, there's no need to send our prayers anywhere, because they already exist everywhere.

3. The third principle implies that the past, present, and future are intimately joined. The Matrix appears to be the container that holds time, providing for a continuity between the choices of our present and the experiences of our future.

Regardless of what we call it or how science and religion define it, it's clear that there's something out there—a force, a field, a presence—that is the great "net" that links us with one another, our world, and a greater power.

If we can truly grasp what the three principles tell us about our relationship to each other, the universe, and ourselves, then the events of our lives take on an entirely new meaning. We become participants rather than victims of forces that we can't see and don't understand. To be in such a place is where our empowerment really begins.

CHAPTER TWO

SHATTERING THE PARADIGM:
THE EXPERIMENTS THAT CHANGE EVERYTHING

*"Everything must be based
on a simple idea. Once we have
finally discovered it, [it] will be
so compelling, so beautiful, that
we will say to one another, yes, how
could it have been any different."*
— John Wheeler (1911–), physicist

*"There are two ways to
be fooled. One is to believe
what isn't true; the other is to
refuse to believe what is true."*
— Søren Kierkegaard (1813–1855),
philosopher

The first rays of the morning sun cast long shadows from the Sangre de Cristo (Blood of Christ) Mountains that towered behind us to the east. I had agreed to meet my friend Joseph (not his real name) there in the valley simply to walk, talk, and enjoy the morning. As we stood on the rim of the vast expanse of land that connects northern New Mexico with southern Colorado, we could see for miles across the fields that separated us from the great gash in the earth, the Rio Grande Gorge, which forms the banks of the Rio Grande. The high-desert sage was especially fragrant that morning, and as we began our walk, Joseph commented on the family of vegetation that covers the land.

"This entire field," he began, "as far as our eyes can see, works together as a single plant." The heat from his breath mixed with the icy morning air, and brief clouds of steam lingered for a few seconds as he formed each word.

"There are many bushes in this valley," he continued, "and every plant is joined to the others through a root system that's beyond our view. Although they're hidden from our eyes beneath the ground, the roots still exist—the entire field is one family of sage. And as with any family," he explained, "the experience of one member is shared to some degree by all others."

I contemplated what Joseph was saying. What a beautiful metaphor for the way we're connected to one another and the world around us. We've been led to think that we're separate from one another, our world, and everything that happens in it. In that belief, we feel isolated, alone, and sometimes powerless to change the things that cause our own pain and the suffering of others. The irony is that we also find ourselves inundated with self-help books and workshops that tell us how connected we are; how powerful our consciousness is; and how humankind is really a single, precious family.

As I listened to Joseph, I couldn't help but think of the way in which the great poet Rumi described our condition. "What strange beings we are!" he said. "That sitting in hell at the bottom of the dark, we're afraid of our own immortality."[1]

Precisely, I thought. *Not only are the plants in this field connected, but they possess a power together that's greater than any of them has alone.* Any single shrub in the valley, for example, influences only the small area of earth that surrounds it. Put hundreds of thousands of them together, though, and you have a power to reckon with! Together, they change features such as the pH of the soil in a way that assures their survival. And in doing so, the by-product of their existence—their abundant oxygen—is the very essence of ours. As a unified family, these plants can change their world.

We may actually have more in common with the sage in that New Mexico valley than you'd think. Just as they have the power individually and collectively to change their world, so do we.

A growing body of research suggests that we're more than cosmic latecomers simply passing through a universe that was completed long ago. Experimental evidence is leading to a conclusion that we're actually creating the universe as we go and adding to what already exists! In other words, we appear to be the very energy that's forming the cosmos, as well as the beings who experience what we're creating. That's because *we are consciousness,* and consciousness appears to be the same "stuff" from which the universe is made.

This is the very essence of quantum theory that troubled Einstein so much. Until the end of his life, he held to a belief that the universe exists independently of us. Responding to analogies about our effect on the world and the experiments showing that matter changes when we observe it, he simply stated, "I like to think that the moon is there even if I am not looking at it."[2]

While our precise role in creation is still not fully understood, experiments in the quantum realm clearly show that consciousness has a direct effect on the most elementary particles of creation. And we are the source of the consciousness. Perhaps John Wheeler, professor emeritus at Princeton and a colleague of Einstein, may have best summarized our newly understood role.

Wheeler's studies have led him to believe that we might live in a world that's actually created by consciousness itself—a process that he calls a *participatory universe.* "According to it [the participatory principle]," says Wheeler, "we could not even imagine a universe that did not somewhere and for some stretch of time contain observers because the very building materials of the universe are these acts of observer-participancy."[3] He offers the central point of quantum theory, stating, "No elementary phenomenon is a phenomenon until it is an observed (or registered) phenomenon."[4]

SPACE IS THE MATRIX

If the "building materials of the universe" are made from ob-servation and participation—*our* observation and *our* participation—what's the stuff that we're creating? To make anything, there must first be something there for us to create with, some malleable essence that's the equivalent of Play-Doh for the universe. What are the universe, the planet, and our bodies made of? How does it all fit together? Do we really have control of anything?

To answer these kinds of questions, we must move beyond the boundaries of our traditional sources of knowledge—science, religion, and spirituality—and marry them into a greater wisdom. This is where the Divine Matrix comes in. It's not that it plays the small role of a by-product in the universe or is simply a part of creation; *the Matrix is creation*. It's both the material that comprises everything as well as the container for all that's created.

When I think of the Matrix in this way, I'm reminded of how University of California at Santa Cruz cosmologist Joel Primack described the instant that creation began. Rather than the big bang being an explosion that happened in one place, in the manner we typically expect explosions to happen, he says, "The big bang did not occur somewhere in space; it occupied the whole of space."[5] The big bang was *space itself* bursting into a new kind of energy, *as* that energy! Just as the origin of the universe was space itself manifesting energetically, the Matrix is *reality itself*—all possibilities, ever moving, as the enduring essence that connects all things.

THE FORCE BEFORE THE BEGINNING

The ancient collection of writings from India called the Vedas are among the world's oldest scriptures and are believed by some scholars to date as far back as 7,000 years. In what's perhaps the best-known text, the Rig Veda, there's a description of a force that underlies creation from which all things are formed—the force that was there before the "beginning." This power, named *Brahman*, is identified as the "unborn . . . in whom all existing things abide."[6] Further in the text it becomes clear that all things exist because "the One manifests as the many, the formless putting on forms."[7]

In different language, we could think of the Divine Matrix in precisely the same way—as the force before other forces. It's the container that holds the universe as well as the blueprint for everything that happens in the physical world. Because it's the substance of the universe, it stands to reason that is has existed since the beginning of creation. If this is the case, then the logical question is: "Why haven't scientists found evidence of the Matrix before now?"

This very good question is one that I ask scientists and researchers investigating this field every opportunity I get. Each time I do so, the response is so similar that I can almost predict what's about to happen. First, there's the look of disbelief that I could in any way imply that science has somehow missed a discovery as important as the field of energy that connects everything in creation. Next, the discussion turns to equipment and technology. "We simply haven't had the technology to detect such a subtle field" is the way the answer usually goes.

While this may have been true at some point, for at least the last hundred years we *have* had the ability to build the detectors that would tell us that the Divine Matrix (or the ether, web of creation, or whatever we choose to call it) exists. It may be more accurate to say that the greatest stumbling block to our discovery of the Divine Matrix has been the reluctance of mainstream science to acknowledge that it's there.

This primal force of energy provides the essence of all that we experience and create. It holds the key to unraveling the deepest mysteries of who we are, as well as to answering the oldest questions about how things work in our world.

THREE EXPERIMENTS THAT CHANGE EVERYTHING

History will look upon the last century as the one of discovery and scientific revolution. Arguably, the key breakthroughs that have become the foundation for entire disciplines have occurred over the course of the last 100 years. From the 1947 discovery of the Dead Sea Scrolls to Watson and Crick's model of the DNA double helix to our ability to miniaturize the electronics for microcomputers, the 20th century was unprecedented in terms of scientific advancement. Many of the findings came so quickly, however, that they left us reeling in their wake. While they opened the door to new possibilities, we weren't yet able to answer the question "What does this new information mean in our lives?"

Just as the 20th century was a time of discovery, we may find that the 21st is a period for making sense of what we've found out. Many of the mainstream scientists, teachers, and researchers of our day are engaged in this process. While the existence of a universal energy field had been theorized, visualized, written about, and imagined for a long while, it's only been recently that experiments were performed proving once and for all that the Matrix exists.

Between 1993 and 2000, a series of unprecedented experiments demonstrated the existence of an underlying field of energy that bathes the universe. For the purpose of this book, I've chosen three that clearly illustrate the kind of studies that are redefining our idea of reality. I emphasize that these are representative experiments only, since others are being reported, seemingly on a daily basis, that offer similar results.

While the studies themselves are fascinating, what really interests me is the thinking behind each investigation. When scientists design experiments to determine the relationship between human DNA and physical matter, for example, we can rest assured that a major paradigm shift is just around the corner. I say this because before these experiments proved that such a relationship exists, the common belief was that everything in our world is separate.

Just as we've heard scientists from the "old school" state clearly that if you can't measure something, it doesn't exist, in a similar vein, prior to the publication of the following experiments, the belief was that if two "somethings" are physically separate in the world, then they have no effect on one another—no connection. But all that changed in the final years of the last century.

It was during this time that quantum biologist Vladimir Poponin reported the research that he and his colleagues, including Peter Gariaev, were doing at the Russian Academy of Sciences. In a paper that appeared in the U.S. in 1995, they described a series of experiments suggesting that human DNA directly affects the physical world through what they believed was a new field of energy connecting the two.[8] My sense is that the field they found themselves working with is probably not really "new" in the truest sense of the word. The more likely scenario is that it's always existed and has simply never been recognized because it's made of a form of energy that we've never had the equipment to measure.

Dr. Poponin was visiting an American institution when this series of experiments was repeated and published. The magnitude of what his study, "The DNA Phantom Effect," tells us about our world is perhaps best summarized in the words of Poponin himself. In the introduction to his report, he says, "We believe this discovery has tremendous significance for the explanation and deeper understandings of the mechanisms underlying subtle energy phenomena including many of the observed alternative healing phenomena."[9]

So what is Poponin really saying to us here? Experiment I describes the phantom effect and what it says about our relationship to our world, one another, and the universe beyond. . . . It's all about our DNA and us.

EXPERIMENT I

Poponin and Gariaev designed their pioneering experiment to test the behavior of DNA on light particles (photons), the quantum "stuff" that our world is made of. They first removed all the air from a specially designed tube, creating what's thought of as a vacuum. Traditionally, the term *vacuum* implies that the container is empty, but even with the air taken out, the scientists knew that something remained inside—photons. Using precisely engineered equipment that could detect the particles, the scientists measured their location within the tube.

They wanted to see if the particles of light were scattered everywhere, clinging to the sides of the glass, or perhaps clustered in a pile at the bottom of the container. What they found first came as no surprise: The photons were distributed in a way that was completely unordered. In other words, the particles were everywhere inside of the container—which is precisely what Poponin and his team expected.

In the next part of the experiment, samples of human DNA were placed inside the closed tube with the photons. In the presence of the DNA, the particles of light did something that no one anticipated: Rather than the scattered pattern that the team had seen before, *the particles arranged themselves* differently in the presence of the living material. The DNA was clearly having a direct influence on the photons, as if shaping them into regular patterns through an invisible force. This is important, since there's absolutely nothing in the tenets of conventional physics that would allow for this effect. Yet in this controlled environment, DNA—the substance that composes us—was observed and documented to have a direct effect on the quantum *stuff that our world is made of!*

The next surprise came when the DNA was removed from the container. There was every reason for the scientists involved to believe that the particles of light would return to their original scattered state throughout the tube. Following the Michelson-Morley experiment (described in Chapter 1), nothing in the traditional literature suggests that anything other than this would happen. But instead, the scientists witnessed a very different occurrence: The photons remained ordered, just as if the DNA were still in the tube. In his own words, Poponin described the light as behaving "surprisingly and counter-intuitively."[10]

After checking the instruments and the results, Poponin and his colleagues were faced with the task of finding an explanation for what they'd just observed. With the DNA removed from the tube, what was affecting the particles of light? Did the DNA leave something behind, a residual force that lingered after the physical material was removed? Or was an even more mysterious phenomenon at work? Were the DNA and the light particles still connected in some way and on some level that we don't recognize, even though they were physically separated and no longer in the same tube?

In his summary, Poponin wrote that he and the researchers were "forced to accept the working hypothesis that some new field structure is being excited."[11] Because the effect appeared to be directly related to the presence of the living material, the phenomenon was named the "DNA phantom effect." Poponin's new field structure sounds surprisingly similar to the "matrix" that Max Planck identified more than 50 years earlier, as well as the effects suggested in ancient traditions.

— **Summary of Experiment I:** This experiment is important for a number of reasons. Perhaps the most obvious is that it clearly shows us a direct relationship between DNA and the energy that our world is made of. Of the many conclusions that we may draw from this powerful demonstration, two are certain:

1. A type of energy exists that has previously gone unrecognized.

2. Cells/DNA influence matter through this form of energy.

Produced under the rigid control of laboratory conditions (perhaps for the first time), evidence arose of the powerful relationship that ancient traditions have held sacred for centuries.

The DNA changed the behavior of the light particles—the essence of our world. Just as our most cherished traditions and spiritual texts have informed us for so long, the experiment validated that we have a direct effect on the world around us.

Beyond wishful thinking and New Age isms, this impact is real. The DNA phantom effect shows us that under the right conditions and with proper equipment, this relationship can be documented. (We'll revisit this experiment in a later part of the book.) Although it stands on its own as a revolutionary and graphic demonstration of the connection between life and matter, it's within the context of the next two experiments that the DNA phantom effect takes on even greater significance.

EXPERIMENT II

Research has shown beyond any reasonable doubt that human emotion has a direct influence on the way our cells function in our body.[12] During the 1990s, scientists working with the U.S. Army investigated whether or not the power of our feelings continues to have an effect on living cells, specifically DNA, once those cells are no longer part of the body. In other words, when tissue samples are taken, does emotion still impact them either positively or negatively?

Conventional wisdom would assume not. Why should we expect such a finding? Refer once again to the Michelson-Morley experiment of 1887, the results of which were believed to show that there's nothing "out there" to connect anything in the world with anything else. Following a traditional line of thinking, once tissue, skin, organs, or bones are removed from a person, any connection with those parts of the body should no longer exist. This experiment, however, shows us that something very different is actually happening.

In a 1993 study reported in the journal *Advances,* the Army performed experiments to determine precisely whether the emotion/DNA connection continues following a separation, and if so, at what distances?[13] The researchers started by collecting a swab of tissue and DNA from the inside of a volunteer's mouth. This sample was isolated and taken to another room in the same building, where they began to investigate a phenomenon that modern science says shouldn't exist. In a specially designed chamber, the DNA was measured electrically to see if it responded to the emotions of the person it came from, the donor who was in another room several hundred feet away.

In his room, the subject was shown a series of video images. Designed to create genuine states of emotion inside of his body, this material ranged from graphic wartime footage to erotic images to comedy. The idea was for the donor to experience a spectrum of real emotions within a brief period of time. While he was doing so, in another room his DNA was measured for its response.

When the donor experienced emotional "peaks" and "dips," his cells and DNA showed a powerful electrical response at the same instant in time. Although distances measured in hundreds of feet separated the donor and the samples, the DNA acted as if it was still physically connected to his body. The question is "Why?"

There's a footnote to this experiment that I'll share here. I was on a book tour in Australia during the September 11 attacks on the American Pentagon and World Trade Center. When I arrived back in Los Angeles, it was immediately clear that I'd come home to a country that was different from the one I'd left only ten days before. No one was traveling—the airports and their parking lots were empty. The world had changed tremendously.

I was scheduled to speak at a conference there in L.A. shortly after returning, and even though it appeared that very few people would show up, the hosts made the decision to go forward with the program. When the presentations began, the producers' fears were realized: Only a handful of attendees had shown up. As the scientists and authors began their talks, it was almost as if we were presenting to one another.

I'd just finished offering my program on the interconnected nature of all things, complete with the Army experiment I just described. At dinner that evening, another presenter came up to me, thanked me for my program, and informed me that he had been a part of the study that I'd spoken of. To be accurate, the man, Dr. Cleve Backster, *had designed* the experiment for the Army as part of an ongoing project. His pioneering work on the way that human intention affects plants had led to the military experiments. What Dr. Backster offered next is the reason why I'm sharing the story here.

The Army stopped their experiments with the donor and his DNA when they were still in the same building, separated by distances of only hundreds of feet. Following those initial studies, however, Dr. Backster described how he and his team had continued the investigations at even greater distances. At one point, a span of 350 miles separated the donor and his cells.

Furthermore, the time between the donor's experience and the cell's response was gauged by an atomic clock located in Colorado. In each experiment, the interval measured between the emotion and the cell's response was zero—*the effect was simultaneous.* Whether the cells were in the same room or separated by hundreds of miles, the results were the same. When the donor had an emotional experience, the DNA reacted as if it were still connected to the donor's body in some way.

While this may sound a little spooky to us at first, consider this: If there's a quantum field that links all matter, then everything must be—and remain—connected. As Dr. Jeffrey Thompson, a colleague of Cleve Backster, states so eloquently, from this viewpoint: "There is no place where one's body actually ends and no place where it begins."[14]

— Summary of Experiment II: The implications of this experiment are vast and, to some, a little mind-boggling. If we can't separate people from the parts of their bodies, does this mean that when a living organ is successfully transplanted into another human being, the two individuals somehow remain connected to each other?

On a typical day, most of us come into contact with dozens, and sometimes hundreds, of other people—and often that contact is physical. Each time we touch another person, even simply by shaking his or her hand, a trace of that individual's DNA stays with us in the form of skin cells that he or she leaves behind. At the same time, some of ours remains with the other person. Does this mean that we continue to be linked to those we touch as long as the DNA in the cells we share is alive? And if so, just how deep does our connection with them go? The answer to these questions is yes—it appears that the link exists. The quality of that connection, however, appears to be determined by how conscious we are of its existence.

All of these possibilities illustrate the magnitude of what this experiment is showing us. At the same time, they lay the foundation for something even more profound. If the donor is experiencing emotions within his or her body and the DNA is responding to those emotions, then something must be traveling between them that allows the emotion to get from one to the other, right?

Perhaps . . . or perhaps not. This experiment could just be showing us something else—a powerful idea that's so simple it's easy to overlook: *Maybe the donor's emotions didn't have to travel at all.* It could be that there's no need for the energy to travel *from* the donor *to* a distant location in order for it to have an effect. The person's emotions might have already been in the DNA—and everywhere else, for that matter—the instant they were created. I mention this here to plant the seed of an amazing possibility that we'll explore with all the consideration that it deserves in Chapter 3.

The bottom line—the reason why I've chosen to share this experiment—is simply this: For the DNA and the donor to have any connection whatsoever, there must be something that links them together. The experiment suggests four things:

1. A previously unrecognized form of energy exists between living tissues.

2. Cells and DNA communicate through this field of energy.

3. Human emotion has a direct influence on living DNA.

4. Distance appears to be of no consequence with regard to the effect.

EXPERIMENT III

While the effect of human emotion on our body's health and immune system has long been accepted in spiritual traditions throughout the world, rarely has it been documented in a way that's useful to the average person.

In 1991, an organization named the Institute of HeartMath was formed for the specific purpose of exploring the power that human feelings have over the body, and the role that those emotions may play in our world. Specifically, HeartMath chose to focus its research on the place in our bodies where emotion and feeling seem to originate: the human heart. The pioneering work of its researchers has been extensively published in prestigious journals and cited in scientific papers.[15]

One of the most significant findings reported by HeartMath is the documentation of the doughnut-shaped field of energy that surrounds the heart and extends beyond the body. This field of electromagnetic energy exists in a configuration called a torus and is between five and eight feet in diameter (see Figure 2). Although the heart field is not the body's aura or the *prana* described in ancient Sanskrit traditions, it may well be an expression of the energy that begins in this area.

Knowing that this field exists, the HeartMath researchers asked themselves if there could be another kind of energy we haven't yet discovered that's carried within this known field. To try out their theory, the researchers decided to test the effects of human emotion on DNA—the essence of life itself.

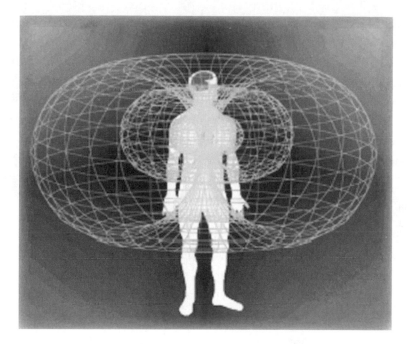

Figure 2. Illustration showing the shape and relative size of the energetic field that surrounds the human heart. (Courtesy of the Institute of HeartMath.)

The experiments were conducted between 1992 and 1995, and began by isolating human DNA in a glass beaker[16] and then exposing it to a powerful form of feeling known as *coherent emotion*. According to Glen Rein and Rollin McCraty, the principal researchers, this physiological state may be created intentionally by "using specially designed mental and emotional self-management techniques which involve intentionally quieting the mind, shifting one's awareness to the heart area and focusing on positive emotions."[17] They performed a series of tests involving up to five people trained in applying coherent emotion. Using special techniques that analyze the DNA both chemically and visually, the researchers could detect any changes that happened.

The results were undeniable and the implications were unmistakable. The bottom line: Human emotion changed the shape of the DNA! Without physically touching it or doing anything other than creating precise feelings in their bodies, the participants were able to influence the DNA molecules in the beaker.

In the first experiment, which involved only one person, effects were produced by a combination of "directed intention, unconditional love and specific imagery of the DNA molecule." In the words of one of the researchers, "These experiments revealed that different intentions produced different effects on the DNA molecule causing it to either wind or unwind."[18] Clearly, the implications are beyond anything that's been allowed for in traditional scientific theory until now.

We've been conditioned to believe that the state of the DNA in our body is a given. Contemporary thinking suggests that it's a fixed quantity—we "get what we get" when we're born—and with the exception of drugs, chemicals, and electrical fields, our DNA doesn't change in response to anything that we can do in our lives. But this experiment shows us that nothing could be further from the truth.

THE INNER TECHNOLOGY TO CHANGE OUR WORLD

So what are these experiments telling us about our relationship to the world? The common denominator among all three is that they involve human DNA. There's absolutely nothing in conventional wisdom that allows for the material of life in our bodies to have any effect whatsoever on our outer world. And there's also nothing to suggest that human emotion can in any way affect DNA when it's *inside* the body of its owner, let alone when it's hundreds of miles away. Yet this is precisely what the results are showing us.

When we think of each experiment on its own, without any consideration of the others, it's interesting. Each one shows us something that appears to be an anomaly existing beyond the bounds of conventional thinking, and some of the findings may even be a little surprising. Without a greater context, we might be tempted to put the experiments into the category of "Things to take another look at on another day . . . one far, far away." But when we consider the three experiments together, something no less than paradigm shattering happens: They begin to tell us a story. When we look at each experiment as a piece of a bigger puzzle, that story jumps out at us like the hidden images of an Escher drawing! So let's look a little deeper. . . .

In the first experiment, Poponin showed us that human DNA has a direct effect on the vibration of light. In the second—the military experiment—we learned that whether we're in the same room with our DNA or separated by distances of hundreds of miles, we're still connected to its molecules, and the effect is the same. In the third experiment, the HeartMath researchers showed us that human emotion has a direct effect on DNA, which in turn directly impacts the stuff our world is made of. This is the beginning of a technology—an *inner* technology—that does more than simply *tell us* we can have an effect on our bodies and our world . . . it *shows us* that this effect exists and how it works!

All these experiments suggest two similar conclusions, which are the crux of this book:

1. There is something "out there": the matrix of an energy that connects any one thing with everything else in the universe. This connective field accounts for the unexpected results of the experiments.

2. The DNA in our bodies gives us access to the energy that connects our universe, and emotion is the key to tapping in to the field.

In addition, the experiments show us that our connection to the field is the essence of our existence. If we understand how it works and the way we're connected to it, then we have all that we need to apply what we know of the field to our lives.

I invite you to think about what these results and conclusions mean in your life. What problem can't be solved, what illness can't be healed, and what condition can't be improved if we're able to tap the force and change the quantum blueprint where all of these things come from? That blueprint is the previously unrecognized field of energy that Max Planck described as the "conscious and intelligent Mind."

THE DiViNE MATRiX

The experiments show that the Matrix is made of an energy form that's unlike any we've ever known in the past—that's why it took so long for scientists to find it. Called "subtle energy," it simply doesn't work the way a typical, conventional electrical field does. Rather, it appears to be a tightly woven *web,* and it makes up the fabric of creation that I'm calling the Divine Matrix.

Figure 3. The experiments suggest that the energy connecting the universe exists as a tightly woven web that makes up the underlying fabric of our reality.

Of the many ways we could define the Divine Matrix, perhaps the simplest is to think of it as being three basic things: (1) the container for the universe to exist within; (2) the bridge between our inner and outer worlds; and (3) the mirror that reflects our everyday thoughts, feelings, emotions, and beliefs.

There are three more attributes that set the Divine Matrix apart from any other energy of its kind. First, it can be described as being everywhere all the time . . . it already exists. Unlike a broadcast from a TV or radio station that has to be created in one place before being sent and received somewhere else, this field seems to be everywhere already.

Second, it appears that this field originated when creation did—with the big bang or whatever we choose to call the "beginning." Obviously, no one was here to tell us what was present before, but physicists believe that the massive release of energy that jolted our universe into existence was the very act of creating space itself.

As the Hymn of Creation from the ancient Rig Veda suggests, before the beginning "not even nothing existed then, no air yet, nor a heaven." As the existence of "nothing" exploded into the "something" of space, the stuff between the nothing was born. We can think of the Divine Matrix as an echo of that moment when time began, as well as a link made of time and space that connects us with the creation of everything. It's the nature of this ever-present connection that allows for the nonlocality of things that exist within the Matrix.

The third characteristic of this field, and perhaps the one that makes it so meaningful in our lives, is that it appears to have "intelligence." In other words, the field *responds* to the power of human emotion. In the language of another time, ancient traditions did their best to share this great secret with us. Inscribed on the temple walls, penned onto timeworn parchments, and engrained into the lives of the people themselves, the instructions that tell us how to communicate with the energy that connects everything were left by those who came before us. Our ancestors tried to show us how to heal our bodies and breathe life into our deepest desires and greatest dreams. It's only now, nearly 5,000 years after the first of those instructions was recorded, that the language of science has rediscovered the very same relationship between our world and us.

The energy found in these experiments (and theorized by others) is so new that scientists have yet to agree on a single term to describe it. Thus, there are many different names that are being used to identify the field that connects everything. Edgar Mitchell, the former *Apollo* astronaut, for example, calls it "Nature's Mind."

Physicist and coauthor of superstring theory Michio Kaku described it as the "Quantum Hologram." While these are modern labels for the cosmic force believed to be responsible for the universe, we find similar themes and even similar words in texts created thousands of years before quantum physics.

Dating to the 4th century, for example, the Gnostic Gospels also used the word *mind* to describe this force and how "from the power of Silence appeared 'a great power, the Mind of the Universe, which manages all things. . . .'"[19] As different as the names sound from one another, all of them appear to be describing the same thing—the living essence that is the fabric of our reality.

It's this mind that Planck made reference to in Florence, Italy, in the mid-20th century. During a lecture he presented in 1944, he made the statement that in all probability was not even fully understood by the scientists of the day. In prophetic words that would be as groundbreaking in the 21st century as they were when he spoke them, Planck said:

> As a man who has devoted his whole life to the most clear-headed science, to the study of matter, I can tell you as the result of my research about the atoms, this much: There is no matter as such! All matter originates and exists only by virtue of a force which brings the particles of an atom to vibration and holds this most minute solar system of the atom together. . . . We must assume behind this force the existence of a conscious and intelligent Mind. This Mind is the matrix of all matter.[20]

Beyond any reasonable doubt, the experiments and discussion of this chapter show us that Planck's matrix exists. Regardless of what we choose to call it or which laws of physics it may or may not conform to, the field that connects everything in creation is real. It's here in this very instant—it exists as you and as me. It's the universe inside of us as well as the one that surrounds us, the quantum bridge between all that's possible in our minds and what becomes real in the world. The matrix of energy that explains why the three experiments work as they do also demonstrates how the positive feelings and prayers *within* us can be so effective in the world *around* us.

But our connection to the Matrix of all matter doesn't stop there . . . it continues into the things that we can't see. The Divine Matrix is everywhere and everything. From the bird that's flying in the air high above us to the cosmic particles that pass through our bodies and homes as if we were empty space, all matter exists within the same container of reality: the Divine Matrix. It's what fills the emptiness between you and the words on this page. It's what *space itself* is made of. When you think about the Matrix and wonder about its location, you can rest assured that wherever space exists, there is also subtle energy.

SO WHAT DOES IT ALL MEAN?

Like the great secret that everyone suspects but rarely talks about, through the Divine Matrix we're all connected in the most intimate way imaginable. But what does that connection really mean? What does it imply to be so deeply enmeshed with our world and one another's lives that we share the pure quantum space where imagination lives and reality is born? If we're truly more than simply casual onlookers watching as our lives and the world "happen" around us, then how much "more" are we?

The previous experiments demonstrate that there's a power within each of us that's unlike any ever created by a machine in a laboratory. It's a force that's not bound by the laws of physics—at least not the ones we understand today. And we don't need a lab experiment to know that this connection exists.

How many times have you gone to call someone on the phone, and found that he or she was already on the line when you picked up the receiver . . . or when you dialed the number, you discovered that the line was busy because your pal was calling you!?

On how many occasions have you found yourself enjoying time with friends in a busy street, mall, or airport, only to have the eerie feeling that you've already been in that place or with those people before, doing exactly what you're doing at that moment?

While these simple examples are fun to talk about, they're more than random coincidences. Although we may not be able to prove scientifically *why* these things happen, we all know that they do. In such moments of connectedness and déjà vu, we find ourselves spontaneously *transcending* the limits imposed by physical laws. In those brief instances, we're reminded that there's probably more to the universe and us than we may consciously acknowledge.

This is the same power that tells us we're more than just observers in this world. The key to experiencing ourselves in this way is to create those experiences intentionally—to have our transcendent insights when we want to have them, rather than just when they seem to "happen." With the exception of a few gifted people among us, there appears to be a very good reason why we're not bilocating, time-traveling, and communicating faster than the laws of physics permit: It all comes down to what we believe about ourselves and our role in the universe. And that's what the next section is all about.

We're creators—and even more than that, we're connected creators. Through the Divine Matrix, we participate in the constant change that gives meaning to life. The question now is less about whether or not we're passive observers and more about how we can intentionally create.

PART II

THE BRIDGE BETWEEN IMAGINATION AND REALITY: HOW THE DiViNE MATRiX WORKS

CHAPTER THREE

ARE WE PASSIVE OBSERVERS
OR POWERFUL CREATORS?

*"So, why is the universe as big as it is?
Because we're here."*
— John Wheeler (1911–), physicist

*"Imagination creates reality. . . .
Man is all imagination."*
— Neville (1905–1972),
visionary and mystic

In 1854, Chief Seattle warned the legislators in Washington, D.C., how the destruction of North America's wilderness had implications that would reach far beyond the current time and threaten the survival of future generations. With a profound wisdom that's as true today as it was in the mid-19th century, the chief reportedly stated, "Man did not weave the web of life—he is merely a strand in it. Whatever he does to the web, he does to himself."[1]

The parallel between Chief Seattle's description of our place in the "web of life" and our connection to (and within) the Divine Matrix is unmistakable. As part of all that we see, we're participants in an ongoing conversation—*a quantum dialogue*—with ourselves, our world, and beyond. Within this cosmic exchange, our feelings, emotions, prayers, and beliefs at each moment represent our speaking to the universe. And everything from the vitality of our bodies to the peace in our world is the universe answering back.

WHAT DOES IT MEAN TO "PARTICIPATE" IN THE UNIVERSE?

As mentioned in the last chapter, physicist John Wheeler suggests that not only do we play a role in what he calls a "participatory universe," but we fulfill the *primary* role. The key to Wheeler's proposition is the word *participatory.* In this type of universe, you and I are part of the equation. We're both catalysts for the events of our lives, as well as the "experiencers" of what we create . . . these things are happening at the same time! We're "part of a universe that is a work in progress." In this unfinished creation, "we are tiny patches of the universe looking at itself—and building itself."[2]

Wheeler's suggestion opens the door to a radical possibility: If consciousness creates, then the universe itself may be the result of this awareness. While Wheeler's views were proposed later in the 20th century, we can't help but think back to Max Planck's 1944 statement that everything exists because of an "intelligent Mind," which he called "the matrix of all matter." The question that begs to be asked here is simply: *What Mind?*

In a participatory universe, the act of focusing our conscious-ness—*of us looking somewhere and examining the world*—is an act of creation in and of itself. We're the ones observing and studying our world. We're the mind (or at least part of a greater mind), as Planck described. Everywhere we look, our consciousness makes something for us to look *at.*

Key 5: The act of focusing our consciousness is an act of creation. Consciousness creates!

In our search to find the smallest particle of matter and our quest to define the edge of the universe, this relationship suggests that we may never find either. No matter how deeply we peer into the quantum world of the atom or how far we reach into the vastness of outer space, the act of us looking with the expectation that something exists may be precisely the force that creates something for us to see.

A participatory universe . . . exactly what would that entail? If consciousness really creates, then how much power do we actually have to change our world? The answer may surprise you.

The 20th-century visionary from Barbados known simply by the name of Neville perhaps best described our ability to make our dreams a reality and bring imagination to life. Through his numerous books and lectures, in terms that are simple yet direct, he shared the great secret of how to navigate the many possibilities of the Divine Matrix. From Neville's perspective, all that we experience—literally everything that happens *to* us or is done *by* us—is the product of our consciousness and absolutely nothing else. He believed that our ability to apply this understanding through the power of imagination is all that stands between us and the miracles of our lives. Just as the Divine Matrix provides the container for the universe, Neville suggested that it's impossible for anything to happen outside the container of consciousness.

How easy it is to think otherwise! Immediately after the terrorist acts of September 11 in New York and Washington, D.C., the questions that everyone was asking were "Why did *they* do this to *us?*" and "What did *we* do to *them?*" We live during a time in history when it's so easy to think of the world in terms of "them" and "us" and wonder how bad things can happen to good people. If there is in fact a single field of energy that connects everything in our world, and if the Divine Matrix works the way the evidence suggests, then there can be no *them* and *us,* only *we.*

From the leaders of nations whom we've learned to fear and hate to the people in other countries who touch our hearts and invite our love, we're all connected in what may be the most intimate way imaginable: through the field of consciousness that's the incubator for our reality. Together, we create the healing or the suffering, the peace or the war. This could very well be the most difficult implication of what the new science is showing us. And it might also be the source of our greatest healing and survival.

Neville's work reminds us that perhaps the biggest error in our worldview is to look to external reasons for life's ups and downs. While there are certainly causes and effects that may lead to the events of every day, they seem to originate from a time and a place that appear completely disconnected with the moment. Neville shares the crux of the greatest mystery regarding our relationship to the world around us: "Man's chief delusion is his conviction that there are causes other than his own state of consciousness."[3] Just what does this mean? It's the practical question that naturally arises when we talk about living in a participatory universe. When we inquire how much power we really have to bring about change in our lives and our world, the answer is simple.

> **Key 6:** We have all the power we need to create all the changes we choose!

This capability is available to us through the way we use the power of our awareness and where we choose to place our focus. In his book *The Power of Awareness*, Neville offers example after example of case histories that clearly illustrate precisely how this works.

One of his most poignant stories has remained with me for years. It involves a man in his 20s who'd been diagnosed with a rare heart condition that his doctors believed was fatal. Married with two small children, he was loved by all who knew him and had every reason in the world to enjoy a long and healthy life. By the time Neville was asked to speak with him, the man had lost a tremendous amount of weight and "shrunk to almost a skeleton."

He was so weak that even conversation was hard for him, but he agreed to simply listen and nod his understanding as Neville shared with him the power of his beliefs.

From the perspective of our participating in a dynamic and evolving universe, there can be only one solution to any problem: a change in attitude and in consciousness. With this in mind, Neville asked the man to experience himself *as if his healing had already taken place.* As the poet William Blake suggested, there's a very fine line between imagination and reality: "Man is all Imagination." Just as physicist David Bohm proposes that this world is a projection of events in a deeper realm of reality, Blake continues, "All that you behold, tho' it appears Without, it is Within, / In your Imagination, of which this World of Mortality is but a Shadow."[4] Through the power of consciously focusing on the things that we create in our imagination, we give them the "nudge" that brings them through the barrier from the unreal to the real.

In a single sentence, Neville explains how he provided the words that would help his new friend accomplish his new way of thinking: "I suggested that in imagination, he see the doctor's face expressing incredulous amazement in finding him recovered, contrary to all reason, from the last stages of an incurable disease, that he see him double-checking in his examination and hear him saying over and over, 'It's a miracle—it's a miracle.'"[5] Well, you can guess the reason why I'm sharing this story: The fellow *did* get better. Months later, the visionary received a letter telling him that the young man had, in fact, made a truly miraculous recovery. Neville later met with him and found that he was enjoying his family and his life in perfect health.

The secret, the man revealed, was that rather than simply wishing *for* his health, since the day of their meeting, he had lived from the "assumption of already being well and healed." And herein we find the secret of propelling our heart's desires from the state of imagination to the reality of our everyday lives: It's our ability to feel as if our dreams have already come to life, our wishes are fulfilled, and our prayers already answered.

In this way, we actively share in what Wheeler called our "participatory universe."

LIVING *FROM* THE ANSWER

There's a subtle yet powerful difference between working *toward* a result and thinking and feeling *from* it. When we work toward something, we embark upon an open-ended and never-ending journey. While we may identify milestones and set goals to get us closer to our accomplishment, in our minds we're always "on our way" to the goal, rather than "in" the experience of achieving it. This is precisely why Neville's admonition that we must "enter the image" of our heart's desire and "think from it" is so powerful in our lives.

In the ancient study of martial arts, we see a beautiful metaphor in the physical world for precisely the way this principle works in consciousness. You've no doubt seen the demonstrations of people trained in these disciplines marrying their powers of concentration and strength into a single moment of intense focus where they're able to perform a feat—such as breaking a concrete block or stack of boards—that would otherwise be impossible for them to achieve. The principle that allows for these displays is the same one that Neville described in his story of the young man's healing.

While there are "tricks" that can sometimes be used in order to do these amazing feats without the spiritual emphasis, when they're authentically performed, the key to success lies in where the martial artists place their attention. When they choose to break a concrete block, for example, the very last thing in their mind is the point of contact where their hand will touch the surface. Just as Neville suggested in his instruction to the dying man, the key is to put our focus in the place of the completed act: the healing *already* accomplished or the brick *already* broken.

Martial artists do this by centering their awareness on a point that's *beyond* the bottom of the block. The only way their hand can be in this place is if they've already passed through the space between them and that point. The fact that the space happens to be occupied by something solid, such as a concrete block, becomes almost secondary. In this way, they're thinking *from* the point of completion, rather than about the difficulty of getting *to* there. They're experiencing the joy of what it feels like to accomplish the act, as opposed to all the things that must occur before they can be successful. This simple example offers a powerful analogy for precisely the way consciousness seems to work.

I experienced this principle personally when I was in my early 20s. It was during that time that the center of my life turned away from working in a copper mill and playing in a rock band—and toward the spiritual focus of an inner power. On the morning of my 21st birthday, I suddenly and unexpectedly found myself drawn to the combination of long-distance running, yoga, meditation, and martial arts. I passionately began to pursue all four together, and they became the "rock" that I clung to whenever it seemed that my world was crumbling around me. One day in the dojo (the martial-arts studio) before our karate class began, I witnessed the power of a concentrated focus unlike anything that I'd ever seen growing up in the heartland of northern Missouri.

On that day, our instructor walked into the room and asked us to do something very different from the form and movement practices that were familiar to us. He explained that he would seat himself in the center of the thick mat where we honed our skills, close his eyes, and go into a meditation. During this exercise, he would stretch his arms out on either side of his body, with his palms open and facedown. He asked us to give him a couple of minutes to "anchor" himself in this T position and then invited us to do anything that we could to move him from his place.

The men in our class outnumbered the women by about two to one, and there had always been a friendly competition between the sexes. On that day, however, there was no such division. Together, we all sat close to our instructor, silent and motionless. We watched as he simply walked to the center of the mat, sat down with his legs crossed, closed his eyes, held out his arms, and changed his breathing pattern. I remember that I was fascinated and observed closely as his chest swelled and shrank, slower and slower with each breath until it was hard to tell that he was breathing at all.

With a nod of agreement, we moved closer and tried to move our instructor from his place. At first, we thought that this was going to be an easy exercise, and only a few of us tried. As we grabbed his arms and legs, we pushed and pulled in different directions with absolutely no success. Amazed, we changed our strategy and gathered on one side of him to use our combined weight to force him in the opposite direction. Still, we couldn't even budge his arms or the fingers on his hands!

After a few moments, he took a deep breath, opened his eyes, and with the gentle humor we'd come to respect, he asked, "What happened? How come I'm still sitting here?" After a big laugh that eased the tension and with a familiar gleam in his eyes, he explained what had just happened.

"When I closed my eyes," he said, "I had a vision that was like a dream, and that dream became my reality. I pictured two mountains, one on either side of my body, and myself on the ground between the peaks." As he spoke, I immediately saw the image in my mind's eye and felt that he was somehow imbuing us with a direct experience of his vision.

"Attached to each of my arms," he continued, "I saw a chain that bound me to the top of each mountain. As long as the chains were there, I was connected to the mountains in a way that nothing could change." Our instructor looked around at the faces that were riveted on each word he was sharing. With a big grin, he concluded, "Not even a classroom full of my best students could change my dream."

Through a brief demonstration in a martial-arts classroom, this beautiful man had just given each of us a direct sense of the power to redefine our relationship to the world. The lesson was less about reacting to what the world was showing us and more about creating our own rules for what we choose to experience.

The secret here is that our instructor was experiencing himself from the perspective that he was already fixed in one place on that mat. In those moments, he was living *from* the outcome of his meditation. Until he chose to break the chains in his imagination, nothing could move him. And that's precisely what we found out.

In Neville's words, the way to accomplish such a feat is to make "your future dream a present fact."[6] In a nonscientific language that sounds almost too straightforward to be true, he tells us precisely how this is done. Please don't be deceived by the simplicity of the visionary's words when he suggests that all we need to do to transform our imagination into reality is to "assume the feeling of our wish fulfilled."[7] In a participatory universe of our making, why should we expect it to be difficult to have the power to create?

MANY POSSIBILITIES/ONE REALITY

Why would the way we think and feel about our world have any effect whatsoever on the events that play out in our lives? How does simply making our "future dream a present fact" change the course of events that are already under way? If it looks as if our world is barreling down the path toward a global war, for example, does that conflict really have to occur? When it seems as though our marriage is about to crumble or that we're destined to live with a debilitating heath condition, does the outcome of these experiences have to happen as predicted?

Or is there another factor—one that's often discounted—that may, in fact, play a powerful role in how we experience the things that have already been set into motion? Does life follow our predictions or meet our expectations? The key to living from the place where our imagination is already fulfilled and our dreams and prayers are already answered is to understand how the possibilities exist to begin with. And to do that we need to return briefly to the central discovery that quantum physics makes about our world.

Quantum physics has been hugely successful in describing the behavior of things that are smaller than the atom—so successful, in fact, that a set of "rules" has been created to describe what we can expect to happen in this tiny invisible world. While the rules are few and simple, they can also sound strange as they describe the things that particles do at the subatomic level. They tell us, for example, that:

- The "laws" of physics are not universal, because on small scales things behave differently from the way they do in the everyday world.

- Energy can express itself either as a wave or a particle, and sometimes as both.

- The consciousness of the observer determines how energy will behave.

As good as these rules are, however, it's important to remember that the equations of quantum physics don't describe the *actual existence* of particles. In other words, the laws can't tell us where the particles are and how they act once they get there. They describe only the *potential* for the particles' existence—that is, where they *may* be, how they *might* behave, and what their properties *could* be like. And all of these characteristics evolve and change over time. These things are significant because we're made of the same particles that the rules are describing. If we can gain insight into the way they function, then maybe we can become aware of greater possibilities for how *we* work.

Herein lies the key to understanding what quantum physics is really saying to us about our power in the universe. Our world, our lives, and our bodies exist as they do because they were chosen (imagined) from the world of quantum possibilities. If we want to change any of these things, we must first see them in a new way—to do so is to pick them from a "soup" of many possibilities. Then, in our world, it seems that only one of those quantum potentials can become what we experience as *our* reality. In my karate instructor's vision, for instance, he observed himself fixed to the mat in a place in time—and he was . . . no one could move him.

Which of the many possibilities becomes real appears to be determined by consciousness and the act of observation. In other words, the object of our attention becomes the reality of our world. This is the area where Einstein himself had a problem with quantum theory, stating, "I think that a particle must have a separate reality independent of the measurements."[8] In this context, the "measurements" are the equivalent of the observer—us.

> **Key 7:** The focus of our awareness becomes the reality of
> our world.

Clearly, our role in the universe is central to the question of why the quantum world works in the way that it appears to. This is precisely why it's important first to understand the "what" of scientific observations so that we can understand how we may apply them in our lives.

The mystery of why we need two sets of rules to describe the world can be traced to an experiment that was first conducted in 1909 by Geoffrey Ingram Taylor, a British physicist. While the experiment is nearly a century old, its results are still the subject of controversy and uncertainty. Since the time of the original experiment, it's been re-created a number of times. Each time the results are identical—and just as mind-boggling.

The experiment, called the "double-slit" experiment, involves projecting things such as quantum particles through a barrier that has two small holes in it and measuring the way that they're detected after they come through the openings. Common sense suggests that when things start out on one side as particles, they would travel throughout the experiment in that form and end as particles as well. The evidence, however, shows that something quite extraordinary happens at some point between the place where the particles begin and where they finish.

Scientists have found that when an electron, for example, passes through the barrier with only one opening available, it behaves in just the way we'd expect it to: It begins and ends its journey as a particle. In doing so, there are no surprises.

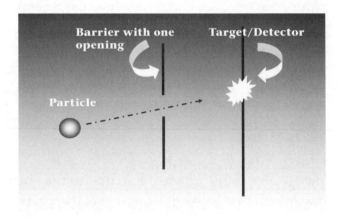

Figure 4. When a single opening is available in the barrier, the particle behaves just as we'd expect.

In contrast, when two slits are used, the same electron does something that sounds impossible. Although it definitely begins its journey as a particle, a mysterious event happens along the way: The electron passes through both slits *at the same time,* as only a wave of energy can do, forming the kind of pattern on the target that only an energy wave can make.

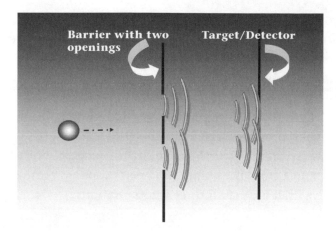

Figure 5. When two openings are available, the particle acts like a wave, passing through both openings at the same time.

This is one example of the kind of behavior that scientists simply have to call "quantum weirdness." The only explanation here is that the second opening has somehow forced the electron to travel *as if* it were a wave yet arrive at its destination just the way it began: as a particle. To do so, the electron has to somehow perceive that the second opening exists and has become available. And this is where the role of consciousness comes in. Because it's assumed that the electron cannot really "know" anything in the truest sense of the word, the only other source of that awareness is the person watching the experiment. The conclusion here is that somehow the knowledge that the electron has two possible paths to move through is in the mind of the observer, and that the onlooker's consciousness is what determines how the electron travels.

The bottom line of the experiment is this: Sometimes the electrons behave just as we would expect. When they do, the rules for our everyday world in which things are distinct and separate seem to apply. At other times, however, the electrons surprise us and act like waves. When this occurs, they require the quantum rules to explain their behavior. And this is where we have the opportunity to see our world and ourselves in a new light, because it means that we're a part of everything, and that consciousness plays a key role in the universe.

Historically, scientists look to one of two main theories to explain the results of the double-slit experiment. Each has its strengths and possesses certain aspects that make more sense than the other explanation. At the time of this writing, both are still theories, and a third possibility has been proposed more recently. Let's take a brief look at all three interpretations.

THE COPENHAGEN INTERPRETATION

In 1927, physicists Niels Bohr and Werner Heisenberg at the Institute for Theoretical Physics in Copenhagen, Denmark, tried to make sense of the quantum weirdness that the new theories were revealing. The result of their work is known as the Copenhagen interpretation. So far, this is the most widely accepted explanation of why quantum particles act as they do.

According to Bohr and Heisenberg, the universe exists as an infinite number of overlapping possibilities. They're all there in a kind of quantum soup with no precise location or state of being until something happens to lock one of the possibilities into place.

That "something" is a person's awareness—the simple act of observation. As the experiment proves, when we look at something such as an electron moving through a slit in the barrier, the very act of observation is what appears to turn one of the quantum possibilities into reality. At that moment, all we see is the version that we've focused on.

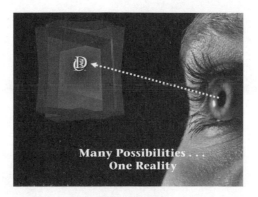

Figure 6. In the Copenhagen interpretation of quantum reality, it's the focus of our consciousness that determines which of the many possibilities (A, B, C, D, and so on) becomes our reality.

Pro: This theory has been tremendously successful in explaining the behavior of quantum particles as they're observed in experiments.

Con: The main criticism of this theory (if it can be can be considered to be one) is that it suggests that the universe can manifest itself only in the presence of someone or something observing it. Additionally, the Copenhagen interpretation doesn't take the factor of gravity into consideration.

THE MANY-WORLDS INTERPRETATION

Following the Copenhagen interpretation, the next most popular explanation for the bizarre behavior of quantum particles is called the many-worlds interpretation of parallel universes. First proposed in 1957 by Princeton University physicist Hugh Everett III, this theory has gained tremendous popularity and support because it seems to address many of the apparent mysteries of the quantum world. Similar to the Copenhagen interpretation, it suggests that at any given moment in time, there are an infinite number of possibilities occurring, and that all of them already exist and are happening simultaneously.

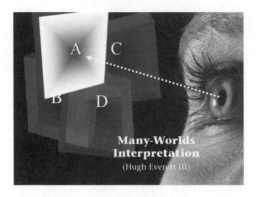

Figure 7. In the many-worlds interpretation of quantum reality, there are an infinite number of possibilities (A, B, C, D, and so on) that already exist. Each possibility exists in its own universe that the other possibilities can't see. As with the Copenhagen interpretation, it's the focus of our consciousness that determines which possibility becomes our reality.

The difference between this and the Copenhagen interpretation is that according to the many-worlds interpretation, each possibility happens in its own space and can't be seen by the others. The unique spaces are called alternate universes. Supposedly, we travel along a timeline of a single possibility in one universe and every once in a while make a quantum leap into another possibility in a different universe. From this perspective, someone could be living a life of illness and disease, and through a shift of focus, suddenly find himself "miraculously" healed while the world around him looks much as it did before.

Everett's interpretation suggests that we already exist in each of these alternate universes. When we take them all into consideration, we live out each and every dream and fantasy that we could ever imagine. Some proponents of this theory even suggest that when we're asleep at night, our dreams are the result of relaxing the focus that keeps us here in our reality, allowing us to drift through other worlds of parallel possibilities. Similar to observers in the Copenhagen interpretation, we only see the possibility we focus on. And that's the key to locking that particular possibility into place as "reality."

Pro: This theory seems to explain why we don't see the many possibilities proposed by the Copenhagen interpretation.

Con: As with any of the ideas based on quantum theory, the theory can't account for the force of gravity. Although it may explain some of what we see in the quantum world, until it can account for *all* of nature's forces, it's seen as incomplete.

In recent years, a third theory has been proposed, one that seems to address the shortcomings of both the Copenhagen and the many-worlds interpretations. Named after its author, Oxford University professor of mathematics Sir Roger Penrose, the Penrose interpretation suggests that the force of gravity that quantum physicists often dismiss is the very thing holding the universe together.

THE PENROSE INTERPRETATION

Similar to the proponents of the other interpretations, Penrose does believe that many possibilities or probabilities exist at the quantum level. His theory differs, however, as to what it is that "locks" one particular possibility into our reality.

Penrose proposes that the quantum possibilities of the other realms are a form of matter. Because all matter creates gravity, each of the possibilities has its own gravitational field. However, it takes energy to maintain this, and the more energy a probability requires, the more unstable it really is. Because it's impossible to sustain enough energy to keep all of them going forever, eventually they collapse into a single state—the most stable one, which we see as our "reality."

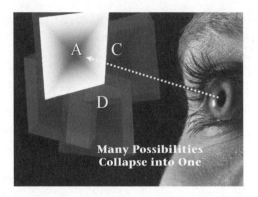

Figure 8. In the Penrose interpretation, there are many possibilities (A, B, C, D, and so on) that eventually collapse into a single reality simply because it requires too much energy to sustain them all indefinitely. While all of the possibilities exist at some point in time, the state that needs the lowest amount of energy is the most stable and the one that we experience as our reality.

Pro: The greatest strength of this theory is that for the first time, it addresses gravity—the one factor that separated Einstein's ideas and the quantum theories—and makes this force central to the existence of reality.

Con: Perhaps the greatest drawback to Penrose's theory (if it can be considered to be one) is that his critics believe that it may not be necessary. Although quantum theory is still only a theory, so far it has been 100 percent successful in predicting the outcome of quantum experiments. So we already have a viable theory for reality. Penrose's interpretation provides this as well, while also including the factor of gravity, which the other theories have failed to do.

SO WHICH ONE IS IT?

Theoretical physicist Michio Kaku, coauthor of the unifying theory of superstrings, may have described the quandary of quantum physics best when he said, "It is often stated that of all the theories proposed in this century, the silliest is quantum theory. Some say that the only thing that quantum theory has going for it, in fact, is that it is unquestionably correct."[9]

Does one of the three prevailing theories explain both the "anomalous" events of the very small subatomic realm and why the world we see works as it does? As good as each interpretation is and as well as it may account for what we notice in the laboratory, the one factor that may be the "missing link" is the role that the Divine Matrix plays in connecting us with the container for all that's observed.

While the onlooker seems to be the wild card in the experiments that produce the unexpected results, what if the "anomalies" aren't anomalies at all? What if the "weirdness" of quantum particles is actually the normal way that matter behaves? Is it possible that everything—from information traveling faster than the speed of light to two things existing in the same place at the same instant in time—is really showing us our potential, rather than our limitations? If so, then we have to ask ourselves: "What's the one factor that links all these things together and prevents us from experiencing the same freedom that quantum particles seem to?"

We're the precise factor that's missing in the existing theories! Specifically, it's our ability to purposefully create the conditions of consciousness (thoughts, feelings, emotions, and beliefs) that lock one possibility of our choosing into the reality of our lives. And this is what brings science full circle with the world's ancient spiritual traditions. Both science and mysticism describe a force that connects everything together and gives us the power to influence how matter behaves—and reality itself—simply through the way we perceive the world around us.

The key is that there's a big difference in the significance that various spiritual traditions and mainstream science give to the discoveries in the quantum world. For reasons that I described earlier, physicists for the most part believe that the way electrons and photons behave has little to do with how we live our everyday lives. The ancient traditions, on the other hand, suggest that it's *because* of the way things work on a subatomic level that we can change our bodies and the world. If this is true, then what happens in the quantum realm has *everything* to do with our day-to-day lives.

As my Native American friend Joseph suggested in the canyon, we don't need machines to create the miraculous effects that we see in quantum particles. Through the power of our forgotten inner technology, we can heal, bilocate, be everywhere at once, remote-view, connect telepathically, choose peace, and do everything in between. It's all about our power to focus consciousness, which is the great secret of some of our most ancient and cherished traditions.

REALITY-MAKING 101

In the teachings of Mahayana Buddhism, it's believed that reality can exist only where our mind creates a focus. In fact, the wisdom suggests that both the world of pure form and that of the formless result from a mode of consciousness called "subjective imagination."[10] While any experience certainly seems real enough to us, it's only when we direct our attention while we're having a feeling about the object of our focus that a possible reality becomes that "real" experience. Except for a slight variation in the language, this ancient tradition sounds a lot like 20th-century quantum theory.

If all of the dos and don'ts of quantum possibilities are true and emotion is the key to choosing reality, then the question is: "How do we feel as if something has happened when the person next to us stares us squarely in the face and says that it hasn't?" For example, are we lying to ourselves if we say that a loved one is already healed while we're standing over that person in the intensive care unit of St. Someone's Hospital?

The irony of this last question is that its very nature eludes any single answer. In a universe of many possible realities, there are numerous potential answers. Somewhere among all those alternate realities there exists a scenario where our loved one's healing has already happened. Someplace there's a reality where the disease never even occurred. For reasons that we may never know or understand, however, this isn't the outcome that's been awakened—it's not the reality that's lying on the gurney in front of us.

The answer to our question boils down to what we believe about the world and our power to choose. The question then becomes: "Which possibility do we pick? Which reality does our loved one or the doctor decide on?" To answer this, we must first acknowledge that we have the power to make such a choice.

Just as Neville's story of the man and his near-fatal illness demonstrated, the present reality isn't set in stone. Rather, it appears to be soft and malleable; it can even change when it looks as if there's no reason for it to do so. In Neville's account, the young man's doctors had made a diagnosis (picked a reality) with an expected outcome. Not knowing that he had a choice, the man initially believed them and bought into their version of reality. It was only when he was offered another possibility *and he accepted it* that his body responded to his new belief—and did so quickly. (I share another powerful example of such a possibility in Chapter 4.)

Einstein made a famous statement that we can't solve a problem while we're in the same level of thinking that created it. Similarly, we can't change a reality if we remain in the same consciousness that made it. To lock in one of the many possibilities described by the Copenhagen, many-worlds, and Penrose theories of reality, we must pinpoint it. And we do so through the way we "observe" it—that is, how we feel about it in our lives.

Once we recognize that we have a choice in terms of *what* we see as our reality, the next questions that are commonly asked are: "How do we do it? How are we to view someone as healed if the body of that person appears diseased?" The answer begins with our willingness to look beyond the illusion of what the world is showing us. In the example of our loved ones' illnesses, we're invited to see beyond the sickness that they've experienced, thinking about them as already healed and feeling what it's like to be with them in this new reality.

To choose a different possibility, however, we must do more than just *think* about the new way of being or *wish* that the recovery of our loved one had already happened. This is perhaps the greatest caution in this way of seeing the world and the one that can present the greatest pitfall. In our fear of losing the people, places, and things that we hold most dear, there's a temptation to deal with the magnitude of the situation by denying the reality that stares us in the face, simply saying that we don't believe it. But unless we also take the *actions* that replace that frightening reality with one of healing, our nonacceptance is bound to produce little more than frustration and disappointment.

I've personally experienced the loss of friends who fell into this trap and are no longer in this world today. Although they're the only ones who'll ever know what really happened in their hearts and minds before passing, I had the opportunity to witness some of the struggles they went through with their beliefs. "If I'm such a powerful being," they reasoned, "then why do I still have this condition? I've changed my beliefs . . . why haven't I healed?"

The topic is deep, personal, and sensitive. And the answer can often bring up strong feelings in discussions about what "is," how the universe seems to work, and where God fits in. The bottom line is this: There's a fine and delicate balance between simply choosing a new possibility and actually following through with the thoughts, feelings, and beliefs that awaken that outcome as a new reality.

Key 8: To simply *say* that we choose a new reality is not enough!

To choose a quantum possibility, we must *become* that way of being. As Neville suggests, we must "abandon" ourselves to the new possibility and in our "love for that state . . . live in the new state and no more in the old state."[11] And that's precisely what the ancient instructions found in some of our most cherished traditions invite us to do. The technique for this human-to-divine interface is often called prayer.

SPEAKING QUANTUM: FEELING IS THE KEY

Earlier in this chapter we identified the various interpretations of why quantum weirdness seems to happen in the way that it does. The theories are particularly concerned with why the act of our simply observing matter seems to change it. While each explanation varied as to *why* the particular effect is happening, they all seem to suggest the same common denominator: us and our role as observers in the world.

When we observe something—that is, when we consciously focus our attention on one place in time—it appears that we're locking one of the many quantum possibilities into place in that instant. Whether it's coming from a "parallel reality" or from the soup of flickering quantum probabilities, the theories suggest that what we see as Reality (with a capital *R*) is what it is because of our presence.

While this appears to be revolutionary news to modern science, it's been accepted as the way things are in ancient traditions and indigenous cultures for centuries. In the words of times past, scribes, mystics, healers, and scholars did their very best to preserve this great secret of our relationship to the universe and pass it on to us. Sometimes we find it in the places where we would least expect to encounter such powerful wisdom.

From the temple walls and tombs in the deserts of Egypt to the Gnostic wisdom of the ancient Nag Hammadi library to the traditional medicine practiced today throughout the American Southwest, the language that breathes life into the possibilities of our imagination, dreams, and prayers remains with us. Perhaps the clearest example of this language is described in the words of a man who lived in a monastery nearly 15,000 feet above sea level, high on the Tibetan plateau.

In the spring of 1998, I had the opportunity to facilitate a combined research trip and pilgrimage into the highlands of central Tibet for 22 days. During that time, the group and I found ourselves immersed in some of the most magnificent, rugged, pristine, and remote land remaining on the planet today. Along the way, we visited 12 monasteries, 2 nunneries, and some of the most beautiful humans that you could ever imagine, including monks, nuns, nomads, and pilgrims. It was during that time that I found myself face-to-face with the abbot of one of the monasteries and got the chance to ask the question that we'd traveled so far and long to ask.

On an icy morning, we found ourselves cramped into a tiny chapel surrounded by Buddhist altars and ancient *thangkas* (the intricately brocaded tapestries that depict the great teachings of the past). I focused my attention directly on the eyes of the timeless-looking man seated lotus-style in front of me. Through our translator, I asked him the same question that I'd asked every monk and nun we'd met throughout our pilgrimage. "When we see your prayers," I began, "what are you doing? When we watch you intone and chant for 14 and 16 hours a day; when we see the bells, bowls, gongs, chimes, mudras, and mantras on the outside, *what's happening to you on the inside?"*

A powerful sensation rippled through my body as the translator shared the abbot's answer. "You've never seen our prayers," he said, "because a prayer cannot be seen." Adjusting the heavy wool robes beneath his feet, the abbot continued, "What you've seen is what we do to create the feeling in our bodies. *Feeling is the prayer!"*

How beautiful, I thought. *And how simple!* Just as the late-20th-century experiments had shown, it's human feeling and emotion that affect the stuff our reality is made of—it's our inner language that changes the atoms, electrons, and photons of the outer world. However, this is less about the actual words we utter and more about the feeling that they create within us. It's the language of emotion that speaks to the quantum forces of the universe . . . feeling is what the Divine Matrix recognizes.

Key 9: Feeling is the language that "speaks" to the Divine Matrix. Feel as though your goal is accomplished and your prayer is already answered.

The abbot was telling us the same thing as the great scientists of the 20th century. Not only was he passing on the same ideas that the experimenters had documented, he was taking it one step further: He was sharing the instructions that describe how we can speak the language of quantum possibilities, and he was doing so through a technique that we know today as a form of prayer. No wonder prayers work miracles! They put us in touch with the pure space where the miracles of our minds become the reality of our world.

COMPASSION: A FORCE OF NATURE AND A HUMAN EXPERIENCE

The clarity of the abbot's answer sent me reeling. His words echoed the ideas that had been recorded in ancient Gnostic and Christian traditions 2,000 years ago. For our prayers to be answered, we must transcend the doubt that often accompanies the positive nature of our desire. Following a brief teaching on overcoming such polarities, the words of Jesus recorded in the Nag Hammadi library remind us of the power of our commands. In words that should be familiar to us by now, we're reminded that when we say to the mountain, "'Mountain move away,' it will move away."[12]

Through the clarity of his words, the abbot answered the mystery of *what* it is the monks and nuns were doing in their prayers: They were speaking the quantum language of feeling and emotion, one that has no words or outer expression.

In 2005, I had the chance to revisit the monasteries of Tibet for a total of 37 days. During the journey, our group learned that the abbot who'd shared the secret of feeling in 1998 had died. Although the circumstances were never made quite clear, we simply knew that he was no longer in this world. Even though we'd never met the man who took his place, when he heard of our return, he welcomed us back and allowed us to continue the conversation that began in 1998.

On another frosty Tibetan morning in a different chapel, we found ourselves face-to-face with the new abbot of the monastery. Only minutes before, we'd been led through the meandering stone-lined passageway that brought us to this tiny, cold, and dimly lit room—in absolute darkness, we'd carefully felt our way one step at a time along the slippery floor, which was dangerously smooth from centuries of spilled yak butter packed onto the surface. It was in the cool, thin air of the ancient room nestled in the heart of this monastery that I asked the new abbot my follow-up questions: "What connects us with one another, our world, and the universe? What's the 'stuff' that carries our prayers beyond our bodies and holds the world together?" The abbot looked directly at me as our translator echoed my question in Tibetan.

Instinctively, I glanced to the guide, who was our go-between for the entire conversation. I wasn't prepared for the translation that I heard coming back to me. "Compassion," he said. "The geshe [great teacher] says that compassion is what connects us."

"How can that be?" I asked, looking for clarity in what I was hearing. "Is he describing compassion as a force of nature or as an emotional experience?" Suddenly, an animated exchange broke out as the translator put my question to the abbot.

"Compassion is what connects all things" was his final answer. And that was it! Following nearly ten minutes of intensive dialogue involving the deepest elements of Tibetan Buddhism, all I got to hear was those six words!

A few days later, I found myself engaged in the same conversation once again, asking the identical question of a high-ranking monk in another monastery. Rather than the formality we experienced in the presence of the abbot, however, we were in the monk's cell—the tiny room where he ate, slept, prayed, and studied when he wasn't in the great chanting hall.

By now, our translator was becoming familiar with the form of my questions and what I was trying to understand. As we huddled around the yak-butter lamps in the dimly lit room, I looked up at the low ceiling. It was covered with black soot from countless years of the same lamps burning for heat and light in the very place where we found ourselves on that afternoon.

Just as I'd asked the abbot only days before, I posed the same question (through the translator) to the monk: "Is compassion a force of creation, or is it an experience?" His eyes turned to the place on the ceiling where I'd been looking only seconds before. Taking a deep sigh, he thought for a moment, collecting the wisdom of what he'd learned since entering the monasteries at the age of eight. (He appeared to be in his mid-20s now.) Suddenly, he lowered his eyes, looking at me as he responded. The answer was short, powerful, and made tremendous sense. "It is both," were the words that came back to me from the monk. "Compassion is *both* a force in the universe as well as a human experience."

On that day, in a monk's cell halfway around the world, nearly 15,000 feet above sea level and hours from even the nearest town, I heard the words of a wisdom that's so simple many Western traditions have overlooked it to this day. The monk had just shared the secret of what connects us to everything in the universe, as well as the quality that makes our feelings and emotions so powerful: They're one and the same.

NOT JUST ANY FEELING WILL DO

Recent translations of ancient prayers recorded in Aramaic, the language of the Essenes (the scribes of the Dead Sea Scrolls) seem to support precisely what the monk was sharing as the secrets of reality making. These new interpretations also offer fresh clues as to why such instructions often appear to be so vague. By retranslating the original New Testament documents, it's clear that tremendous liberties were taken over the centuries with the ancient authors' words and intent. As the saying goes, a lot was "lost in the translation." (I described this—and other examples that I share in these pages—in my last book, *Secrets of the Lost Mode of Prayer,* but they're so relevant that I decided to include them here, too.)

Relating to our ability to participate in the events of life, health, and family, a comparison of the modern biblical version of "Ask and you shall receive," for example, with its original text gives us an idea of just how much can be lost! The modern and condensed King James Version of the Bible reads:

> *"Whatsoever ye ask the Father in my name,*
> *he will give it to you. Hitherto have ye asked*
> *nothing in my name: Ask and ye shall*
> *receive, that your joy may be full."*[13]

When we compare this with the original text, we see the key that's left out. In the following paragraph, I've emphasized the missing part by underlining it.

> *"All things that you ask straightly, directly . . .*
> *from inside My name—*
> *you will be given. So far you haven't done this. . . .*
> *So ask without hidden motive and*
> *be surrounded by your answer—*
> *Be enveloped by what you desire, that your gladness be full."*[14]

With these words, we're reminded of the quantum principle telling us that feeling is a language to direct and focus our consciousness. It's a state of being that we're *in,* rather than something that we *do* at a certain time of day.

While it's clear that emotion is the language that the Divine Matrix recognizes, it's also apparent that not just any feeling will do. If it did, then the world would be a very confusing place, with one person's idea of what should be overlapping with someone else's very different conception. The monk stated that compassion is both a force of creation and the experience that accesses it. The deepest elements of the teaching suggest that in order to achieve compassion, we must approach a circumstance without a strong expectation of the rightness or wrongness of that situation's outcome. In other words, we must perceive it without judgment or ego. And it appears to be precisely this quality of emotion that's the key to speaking to the Divine Matrix in a way that's meaningful and effective.

As the physicist Amit Goswami suggests, it takes more than a regular state of consciousness to make a quantum possibility a present reality. In fact, to do so he indicates that we must be in what he describes as a "non-ordinary state of consciousness."[15]

To get to this point, the Aramaic translation states that we must "ask without hidden motive." Another way of clarifying this very important part of the instruction is to say in modern terms that we must make our decisions from a desire that's *not based in our ego*. The great secret to bringing the focus of our imagination, beliefs, healing, and peace into a present reality is that we must do so without a strong attachment to the outcome of our choice. In other words, we're invited to pray without our judgments of what should or shouldn't be happening.

Key 10: Not just any feeling will do. The ones that create must be without ego and judgment.

Perhaps one of the best descriptions of how we experience this neutral place is found in the work of the great Sufi poet Rumi. With words that are simple and powerful, he states, "Out beyond ideas of wrong-doing and right-doing there is a field. I'll meet you there."[16] How often can we truly say that we're in Rumi's field of nonjudgment at any time in our lives—especially when the fate of our loved ones is hanging in the balance? Yet this appears to be precisely the greatest lesson of our power, the biggest challenge of our lives, and the enormous irony of our ability to create in a participatory universe.

It seems that the *stronger our desire* is to change our world, the *more elusive our power* to do so becomes. This is because what we want is so often ego based. If it weren't, the change wouldn't hold such significance for us. As we mature into the state of consciousness where we *know* that we can alter our reality, however, it also seems that it becomes less important for us to do so.

Similar to the way our desire to drive a car, for example, wanes after we actually begin to do so, in having the ability to work miracles of healing and peace, the urgency to make them happen seems to disappear. This may be because along with knowing that we can change things comes an acceptance of the world just the way it is.

It's this freedom of possessing power without attaching so much importance to it that allows us to be even more effective in our prayers. And herein may lie the answer to the question asked by those who meditated, chanted, *om*ed, danced, and prayed for the recovery of their loved ones.

Although every act was undoubtedly well intentioned, it often involved a strong attachment to having or making the healing of our loved ones happen. It entailed a belief that a miraculous recovery was necessary. And if the healing still *needed* to occur, the implication was that it hadn't taken place yet—if it had, we wouldn't be asking for it in our prayers. It's as if by wanting the outcome of healing, the efforts to create it actually reinforced the reality that the disease was present! This leads to the second part of the ancient instruction, something that's often overlooked in our attempts to bring miracles into our lives.

The next part of the translation invites us to "be surrounded" by our answer and "be enveloped" by what we desire so that our joy may come to pass. This passage reminds us in words of precisely what the experiments and the ancient traditions suggest in their shared wisdom. We must first have the *feeling* of healing, abundance, peace, and the answers to our prayers of well-being in our hearts *as if they've already happened* before they become the reality of our lives.

In the passage, Jesus suggests that those he's speaking with haven't done that. Just like my friends with the powerful medicine of prayer and good intentions, while they may have *believed* that they asked for their prayers to be answered, if their request was simply the words *Please let this healing happen,* then he says that this isn't a language that the universal field of the Divine Matrix recognizes. Jesus reminds his disciples that they must "speak" to the universe in a way that's meaningful. When we *feel* as though we're surrounded by healing in our loved ones and enveloped by peace in our world, that's both the language and the code that opens the door to all possibilities.

In this feeling, we move from the viewpoint that *suspects* we're simply experiencing whatever comes our way to the perspective that *knows* we're part of all that is. Thus, we create a shift of energy that may be described as the classic "quantum leap." In much the same way that an atom's electron jumps from one energy level to another without moving through the space between, when we really know that we're speaking the quantum language of choice and not simply thinking that we might be, we're in another state of consciousness. It's this state that becomes the *pure space* where dreams, prayers, and miracles begin.

WE'RE WIRED TO CREATE

During a conversation with the Indian poet and mystic Rabindranath Tagore in 1930, Albert Einstein summarized the two viewpoints of the early 20th century regarding our role in the universe. "There are two different conceptions about the nature of the universe," he began. The first sees "the world as a unity *dependent* on humanity," and the second perceives "the world as a reality *independent* of the human factor" [author's italics].[17] While the experiments described in Chapter 2 certainly show that our conscious observation of the stuff our world is made of, including atoms and electrons, directly affects the way that matter behaves, we'll probably find that there's a third possibility—one that falls somewhere between Einstein's two extremes.

This possibility may show that our universe came into existence through a process that didn't involve us initially. Although creation could have started without our presence, we're here now as it continues to grow and evolve. From the stars so distant that their lives are over before their light ever reaches our eyes to energy that's disappearing into the mysterious vortices we simply call "black holes," change is the universal constant that we can count on. It's happening as part of everything we see and even in the realms we don't.

By now it should be clear that it's impossible for us to be simply bystanders in our world. As conscious observers, we're part of all that we see. Additionally, although scientists have yet to agree upon which theory explains the *way* we change our reality, they all suggest that the universe is altered in our presence. It's as if being conscious is an act of creation unto itself. As physicist John Wheeler stated, we live in a "participatory" universe—not one where we manipulate or force our will or are able to completely control the world around us.

In our capacity as part of the universe today, we have the ability to modify and change little pieces of it through the way we live our lives. In the realm of quantum possibilities, we appear to be made to participate in our creation. We're wired to create! Because we appear to be universally joined on the quantum level, ultimately our connectedness promises that the seemingly little shifts in our lives can have a huge influence on our world and even the universe beyond. Our quantum link with the cosmos runs so deep that scientists have created a new vocabulary to describe what such connections really mean. The "butterfly effect" mentioned in Chapter 1, for example, describes how small changes can have really big effects.

Formally known as *sensitive dependence on initial conditions,* the bottom line of this phenomenon suggests that a single small change in one part of the world can be the trigger for a huge alteration in another place and time. It's most often stated as the analogy "If a butterfly flaps it wings in Tokyo, then a month later it may cause a hurricane in Brazil."[18] An often-used example of this effect is the result of a turn down the wrong street by Archduke Ferdinand's driver in 1914. This mistake brought the leader of Austria face-to-face with his assassin, and history shows that Ferdinand's death was the catalyst that led to World War I. It all began with the chance occurrence of a simple error that we've all made at one time or another. That wrong turn, however, had global consequences.

In Chapter 2, we explored three experiments that told the story of our relationship to the world around us. They showed us that DNA changes the stuff our world is made of and that emotion alters the DNA itself. The military experiments and those conducted by Cleve Backster demonstrated that this effect isn't limited by time or distance. The net result suggests that you and I direct a force within us that works in a realm that's free from the limits of physics as we know them.

The studies imply that we aren't bound by the scientific laws as we understand them today. This may be precisely the power that the mystic St. Francis alluded to more than 600 years ago when he said, "There are beautiful and wild forces within us."

If there's a power within us to alter the essence of the universe in ways that can heal and create peace, then it makes tremendous sense that there would be a language that allows us to do so consciously and at will. And there is—interestingly, it's precisely the language of emotion, imagination, and prayer that was lost to the West through the Christian church's biblical edits of the 4th century.

WHEN THE MIRACLE STOPS WORKING

The effects of the mind-body connection and certain kinds of prayer are well documented in the open literature. From studies in major universities and field tests in war-torn countries, it's clear that the way we feel within our bodies affects not only us, but the world beyond.[19] This relationship between our inner and outer experiences appears to be the reason some forms of prayer empower us as they do. While the precise mechanism that explains *why* prayers work may not be fully understood, they do and the evidence is there. However, there's also a lingering mystery. In the studies, the positive impact of the prayers seems to last only for the period of time that they're occurring. When they stop, their effects also seem to end.

For example, during experiments in prayers for peace, the studies clearly show that there were statistically significant declines in the key indicators that the researchers were observing. The incidence of traffic accidents, hospital emergency-room visits, and even violent crimes against people went down. In the presence of peace, all that could happen was peace. As interesting as these results are, however, what they demonstrate next has been an ongoing mystery to those studying this effect.[20]

When the experiments stopped, the violence returned, in some instances reaching levels even greater than before the experiments began. What happened? Why did the effects of the meditations and prayers appear to end? The answer to these questions may be the key to understanding the quality of awareness that creates. What happened was that the trainees *stopped* what they were doing—they ceased their meditations and prayers. And this is the answer to our mystery.

If we believe that choosing our reality is something that we do only for the moment, then it makes perfect sense that when we stop feeling as if our new reality exists, the effect of our decision is over as well. Our reality making may be a short-lived choice if we assume that feelings of healing, peace, and abundance are experiences that only last for minutes at a time. Between the modern experiments and the instructions in ancient texts, we know that reality making is more than what we *do* . . . it's what we *are!*

> **Key 11:** We must *become* in our lives the things that we choose to *experience* as our world.

If feeling is the way we choose and we're feeling all the time, then we're also constantly choosing. We can feel our gratitude for the peace in our world with conviction because it always exists somewhere. We can feel appreciation for the well-being of our loved ones as well as ourselves because we're healed and renewed to some degree every day.

This may be precisely what the Aramaic versions of the Gospels were trying to convey to the people of the future through the language that they left for us nearly 2,000 years ago. It may be this very effect that's described in the Gnostic text of the lost Gospel of Thomas, as well: "That which you have will save you if you bring it forth from yourselves. That which you do not have within you [will] kill you if you do not have it within you."[21]

Although the admonition is brief, the implication is powerful. Through the words attributed to the master, Jesus, we're reminded that the power to shape our lives and world is something that lives inside of us as an ability that we all share.

LIFE DOESN'T ALWAYS FOLLOW THE RULES OF PHYSICS

What happens if we live in a way that breaks the accepted rules of physics? Or what if we don't even know the rules exist? Is it possible that we can follow the example of quantum particles that seem to do precisely this?

Common sense tells us that if something exists in one location, then it certainly can't be somewhere else at the same time, regardless of what "it" is. Yet that's precisely what the experiments have shown.

The obvious question that follows such discoveries is: If the stuff that the world is made of can be in two places at once and we're part of the world, then why can't we do the same thing? Why can't we fulfill our duty in the workplace or classroom and at the same time be enjoying ourselves on a sunny beach or hiking through a mountain canyon somewhere? While we've all wondered from time to time if such a thing could occur, the possibility is really just pure fantasy . . . isn't it?

When we hear of something unusual happening on many occasions involving different individuals, there's normally some truth to the reports. While the specifics may vary, it's often possible to trace the underlying theme to an actual event in time. The Great Flood is a perfect example of what I mean here. Throughout history and in a multitude of cultures, there's an almost universal theme that's recounted time and again. Playing out on various continents, in diverse languages, and with different people, the story and the outcome are nearly identical.

Although the details vary, history is similarly punctuated with reports of people who've bilocated—that is, they physically appeared in different locations at the same instant in time. Often these feats are attributed to yogis, mystics, or individuals who have in some way mastered a dormant ability (not always, however). The common thread that seems to link these reports is that those who do the bilocating are generally masters of the power of human emotions such as love and compassion. Frequently, the reports are associated with the holy works of saints and are well documented by missionaries, native peoples, and others who are believed to be reliable witnesses to the miracles.

Among the best documented of the many instances of bilocation attributed to St. Francis of Paola, for example, was a case that happened in 1507. As the holy man was fulfilling his duties at the church altar, people who had come to see him found that he looked as if he was in a deep state of prayer, and they decided not to disturb him. When they left, however, they were more than surprised to find him outside of the church they'd just entered. And he wasn't simply standing there alone; he was talking with locals and those passing by on the street. Quickly, they ran back into the chapel, only to find that he'd never left—he was still there, "lost in prayer." Somehow, through a mysterious state of consciousness associated with a deep meditative state, St. Francis of Paola had appeared to the same people in two locations during the same period of time.

Between 1620 and 1631, María de Agreda, a nun who lived for 46 years in a convent in Agreda, Spain, reported more than 500 journeys across the ocean, away to a distant land. As far as those who knew her and lived with her were concerned, she never once left the convent. For María, however, she would "fly" to the faraway place she spoke of during what she called her "experiences of ecstasy."

Such a phenomenon could be chalked up today to a 300-year-old report of remote viewing (the ability to witness and perceive events from a distance by directing consciousness to a precise location), except for one curious distinction: María de Agreda not only visited the lands that she described, but she taught the indigenous people she encountered there about the life of Jesus. Although she spoke only her native Spanish, the Indians could understand her as she shared the teachings of the great master with them.

The documentation of her sightings came when the archbishop of Mexico, Don Francisco Manzo y Zuniga, heard about her experience. When he sent missionaries to investigate, they were amazed to find that the local Indians of the area were already well educated in the life of Jesus—so well, in fact, that they immediately baptized the entire tribe on the spot.

Nearly a decade later, María de Agreda's mystical journeys were finally validated. While she was under a church-ordered oath of obedience, she described the intimate details of a land that she'd never physically visited. Her description was so complete that she included the subtleties of climate and changing seasons, as well as nuances of the culture and the beliefs of the people whom she'd taught. Following a "rigorous ecclesiastical examination," María de Agreda's mystical journeys were declared by the church to be authentic and she was given the consideration of "the highest rank among the mystics of past ages."[22]

Not all reports of bilocation are from the murky years of the 16th and 17th centuries. As recently as World War II, there have been many instances of holy men appearing in multiple places at once. One of the best documented is that of Italy's mystical Padre Pio. Following his promise that the Nazi-occupied city of San Giovanni Rotondo would be spared from destruction by the Allies, he appeared in broad daylight in a way that's rare even for bilocation.

As the bombers arrived over the city to target German strongholds, the image of Padre Pio in brown robes appeared in front of their planes, hovering in midair! Unlike the brief apparitions that are sometimes reported under the stress of battlefield conditions, the image lingered for all to see. And as long as it remained, any attempt to release bombs on the city failed.

Frustrated and mystified, the pilots changed course and landed their planes at a nearby airfield with all of the bombs that were with them when they began their mission. Shortly afterward, one of the pilots went to a nearby chapel. To his amazement, inside of it he found the same friar that he'd seen earlier hovering in front of his plane . . . it was Padre Pio!

The padre wasn't a ghost or the apparition of a long-deceased saint, as the pilot had suspected. He was real. He was alive. And on that day, he'd somehow been in two places at the same time: on the ground in the chapel and in the air directly in front of the planes. While the Allies liberated Italy, the city of San Giovanni Rotondo was spared, just as Padre Pio had promised.[23]

When we experience something that appears to happen beyond the realm of what we know to be true, we often credit it as a miracle. So what are we to make of the reports and documented cases of bilocation and other seemingly miraculous feats that span more than 600 years? Can we write them off as pure fantasy or wishful thinking? . . . Possibly. There's always the chance that they were conjured up by people with too much time on their hands or who honestly wanted them to be true.

However, what if there's something more happening here? If it's proven to us beyond any doubt that we aren't limited by the current laws of physics, that confirmation allows us to see ourselves in a powerful new light by offering us something beyond faith upon which to base our new beliefs.

Just as the initiates mentioned in the poem in the Introduction to this book found a new freedom in their unexpected experiences, if we find that we can follow in the "footsteps" of quantum particles that operate beyond the boundaries of space and time, then we can certainly use our ability to heal our bodies and bring joy to our lives. The key is this: To do what *seems* to be impossible, one person first has to push the limits of what we previously thought to be true. Just as the initiates discovered that they were more than they'd formerly believed once they moved beyond their fear of "the edge," in order to live miracles in our lives, we must first overcome our beliefs that such phenomena are impossible.

Key 12: We are not bound by the laws of physics as we know them today.

For us to do so, someone must perform that miracle first so that we can see it happen. Maybe that person is particularly gifted in one area of life, such as healing. Or perhaps that individual simply has the openness to see the world differently. Regardless of how it happens, once one person does that special something—whether it's Jesus or your next-door neighbor—then the same miracle becomes available to everyone else.

A beautiful example of this principle is illustrated by the inability of the native peoples of North America to see the ships of the early Europeans that were anchored just off their shores. The concept of a massive wooden boat with huge masts and sails was so foreign to them that they had no point of reference for what they were seeing. In the same way that our vision is capable of detecting the individual frames of a movie, the natives' eyes could certainly make out the silhouette of the ships on the horizon. And just as our brains try to make sense of what we see by merging the frames together into the continuous experience of the movie, the natives tried to do the same thing. The problem was that no one had ever done it before: Nothing in their collective experience told them how to see a European sailing vessel.

It was only when the medicine man of the tribe squinted and used his vision a little differently that he could begin to make out the ships. Once he did, it wasn't long before everyone in the group was able to see what only hours before had been invisible. It was all about the way the people allowed themselves to perceive. In their willingness to try something different, a whole new world opened up to them. Maybe we're not so different from those natives on the shore a little more than 500 years ago. We can only imagine what's in store for us when we think of our world, our universe, and ourselves a little differently.

At the beginning of this section, we asked the question "If an electron is able to be in two places, why can't we?" Perhaps the answer could be found if we posed our query a little differently. Rather than buying into the belief that particles can do something that we can't, let's ask what it takes for an electron to bilocate. If we understand how the stuff we're made of behaves under the circumstances of a miracle, maybe we can find those conditions in our own lives. And to understand how this works, we'll need to explore the single facet of our existence that gives each of us the ability to alter our world by changing ourselves: the power of the hologram.

CHAPTER FOUR

ONCE CONNECTED, ALWAYS CONNECTED: LIVING IN A HOLOGRAPHIC UNIVERSE

*"So here we are—all part of this
great hologram called Creation,
which is everybody else's SELF. . . .
It's all a cosmic play, and
there is nothing but you!"*
— Itzhak Bentov (1923–1979),
scientist, author, and mystic

*To see a world in a grain of sand,
And Heaven in a wild flower,
Hold infinity in the palm of your hand,
And eternity in an hour.*
— William Blake (1757–1827),
poet and visionary mystic

A mystery was alluded to in the experiments of the last section, one that was never solved. A part of the proof that the Divine Matrix actually exists was offered when two "somethings" that were once joined (two photons, the DNA and the photons, or the donor and his DNA) *acted* as if they were still connected to one another, even though they were separated by distances ranging from feet to hundreds of miles. The question is: *Why?*

IS IT REAL, OR IS IT A HOLOGRAM?

We've all heard that a picture is worth a thousand words. As a visual person, I know that this is true for me. For example, seeing one demonstration of *how* to start the engine of my truck is much more meaningful to me than reading all the pages of a manual describing *why* the pistons move and the spark plugs spark when I turn the key! Once I see the big picture, then I can always go back in order to understand the details, if they're even still important; sometimes I just want my truck to start.

I suspect that many of us work in this way. Although we find ourselves in the high-tech world of how-to manuals and computer tutorials about *why* something is the way it is, a direct experience is still the best way to explain a new idea clearly. A powerful example of such an experience is our introduction to the idea of a hologram. Holograms have been used in research since their discovery in the late 1940s.[1] Since that time, however, precisely what one is and how it works had little meaning to the average nontechnical person—until the original *Star Wars* motion picture was released in 1977.

In a pivotal scene early in the film, we see the representative of an entire planet, Princess Leia, pleading for help to save her people. She encodes her message in the form of a digital hologram stored in the memory of R2-D2, the android who captured the hearts and imaginations of audiences throughout the world.

While Princess Leia remains in one part of the universe, R2-D2 carries her holographic image to another world in a galaxy far, far away. The message remained secret until a young warrior, Luke Skywalker, coaxes it from him. In a stunning display of state-of-the-art motion-picture graphics, R2-D2 delivers the Princess's request by projecting a miniature image of her into the room, as if she were there in person.

Suddenly, her lifelike image appears in midair to make the plea. Because she looks three-dimensional to the movie audience, we're given the feeling that if we were there, we'd be able to reach out and touch her just the way we could the person sitting next to us in the theater. If we did so, however, our hands would pass through empty air: She's just a hologram.

For many people in the '70s, this scene was their first experience of a holographic projection and how real it can appear. It also gave us a surprising glimpse of what our phone calls may look like at some point in the not-so-distant future. Even today, decades later, the mere mention of the word *hologram* still brings to mind the image of Princess Leia.

For all intents and purposes, a hologram is generally thought of as a picture—a three-dimensional image—that looks lifelike when it's projected in a particular way or is seen in a certain kind of light. While the film rendition is one example of what the hologram may produce, there's much more to it than simply a photograph.

The holographic principle may be one of the simplest yet least understood phenomena of nature. At the same time, it could hold the greatest potential for making change on even the largest-possible scales within a time frame that's dizzying to the mind. To apply this power in our personal lives, however, we must understand precisely what a hologram is and how it works. So, first things first: Just what *is* a hologram?

UNDERSTANDING THE HOLOGRAM

If you were to ask scientists to explain a hologram, they would probably begin by describing it as a special kind of photograph where the image on the surface suddenly appears three-dimensional when it's exposed to direct light. The process that creates these images involves a way of using laser light so that the picture becomes distributed over the entire surface of the film. It's this property of "distributedness" that makes the holographic film so unique.

In this way, every part of the surface contains the entire image just as it was originally seen, only on a smaller scale. In other words, each fragment is a hologram. If the original picture were divided into any number of pieces, each one—no matter how small—would still show a full view of the entire original image.

Figure 9. When something is holographic, it exists wholly within every fragment of itself, no matter how many pieces it's divided into. This illustration helps convey the idea that no matter how finely we divide the universe—from the four parts shown above to a galaxy, a human, or an atom—each segment mirrors the whole universe, only on a smaller scale.

Just as the direct experience of starting a car's engine is the most effective way to show how it operates, probably the best method of illustrating how a hologram works is also through an example.

Back in the 1980s, a series of bookmarks appeared on the market (which are now collector's items) using holographic technology. Each one was made of a shiny strip of silver paper that looked like glossy aluminum foil at first glance. When the paper was held directly under a bright light and tilted back and forth, however, something happened that set these bookmarks apart from more traditional ones: Suddenly, the images in the foil looked as though they'd come to life and were hovering in the air just above the paper itself. As the bookmark was tilted one way, then another, the image remained present, three-dimensional and lifelike. I remember a number of different versions of these: the face of Jesus, the body of Mother Mary, a dolphin jumping over a pyramid, and a rosebud in full bloom.

If you have one of these bookmarks, you can do an experiment to demonstrate for yourself just how a hologram works. A word of caution here: The drawback is that your bookmark will be destroyed in the process! With this in mind, use a sharp pair of scissors to cut your beautiful, shiny bookmark into hundreds of pieces of any shape. Then, take the smallest of the fragments and cut it again into an even tinier piece. If the bookmark is truly a hologram, you'll be able to look at your tiny speck of a bookmark under a magnifying glass and still see the entire image, only on a smaller scale. The reason why is that it exists everywhere throughout the bookmark.

Key 13: In a holographic "something," every piece of the something mirrors the whole something.

SOLVING THE MYSTERY OF THE TWIN PHOTONS

So, with a clearer understanding of what a hologram is and how it's created, let's revisit the University of Geneva experiment from Chapter 1. To recap: A distance of 14 miles separated twin photons. When one of them was forced to choose between two pathways at the end of its journey, the second photon always made exactly the same choice, as if it "knew" what its twin was doing. The same experiment has been repeated on different occasions, and each time the results are identical. The two particles act *as if* they're still connected, even though they're miles apart.

Conventional wisdom suggests that for this kind of connection to happen, the photons are somehow sending signals to one another. This is where a problem comes in for physicists: For a message to travel between them, it would have to be moving *faster* than the speed of light. But according to Einstein's theory of relativity, nothing can travel that quickly.

So is it possible that these particles are violating the laws of physics . . . or are they demonstrating something else to us? Could they be showing us something so foreign to the way we think about our world that we're still trying to force the mystery of what we see into the comfortable familiarity of how we believe energy gets from one place to another?

What if the signal from one photon never traveled to reach the other? Is it possible that we live in a universe where the information between photons, the prayer for our loved ones, or the desire for peace in a place halfway around the world never needs to be transported anywhere to be received?

The answer is yes! This appears to be precisely the kind of universe we live in. Russell Targ, cofounder of the cognitive-sciences program at the Stanford Research Institute in Menlo Park, California, eloquently and beautifully describes this connection: "We live in a nonlocal world where things physically separated from one another can, nonetheless, be in instantaneous communication."[2] Targ clarifies what such a connection means, stating, "It's not that I close my eyes and send a message to a person a thousand miles away, but rather in some sense there is no separation between my consciousness and his consciousness."[3] The reason why the signals didn't have to travel between photons is because they were already there—they never left *from* anywhere and were never carried *to* another location in the conventional sense.

By definition, every place in a hologram is a reflection of every other. And a property that exists anywhere within it also exists everywhere else. So in the nonlocal hologram of our universe, the underlying energy that links all things instantly connects them as well. Spiritual teachers generally agree with scientists on this view of reality. As Ervin Laszlo, the founder of systems philosophy, describes, "Life evolves, as does the universe itself, in a 'sacred dance' with an underlying field."[4]

This seems to be precisely what the ancient Avata Saka Sutra of Mahayana Buddhism is describing as the "wonderful net" of energy that connects all things in the cosmos. If the universe is nonlocal and holographic, not only does this net link everything together, each point within it also reflects all others. The Sutra begins by stating that at one time in the distant past, this net was "hung" so that "it stretches out infinitely in all directions" as the universe itself.

In addition to *being* the universe, the net contains it and gives it holographic qualities. The ancient Sutra describes an infinite number of jewels throughout the net that serve as cosmic eyes. Thus, all things are visible to all other things. In what may well be the oldest known description of a hologram discovered so far, the Sutra then reveals the power of each jewel to create change throughout the entire net: "Each of the jewels reflected in this one jewel is also reflecting all the other jewels, so that there is an infinite reflecting process occurring."[5] According to the translation of the Sutra I've referenced, this net "symbolizes a cosmos in which there is an infinitely repeated interrelationship among all the members of the cosmos."[6]

What a beautiful description of the subtle yet powerful principle that nature uses to survive, grow, and evolve. In a holographic universe, where each piece already has the whole world mirrored on a smaller scale, all things are already everywhere. The holographic principle promises that everything we need to survive and grow is always with us, everywhere, all the time . . . from the simplicity of a single blade of grass to the complexity of our bodies.

As we understand the power of our infinitely connected hologram, it becomes clear that nothing is hidden and there are no secrets—these things are by-products of our sense of separateness. While it may look as though we're disconnected from one another and the rest of the world, that detachment doesn't exist on the plane where the hologram originates: within the Divine Matrix. On this level of unity, there really can be no such things as "here" and "there."

Now we can answer the "why" of the mysteries in our experiments from the first part of this book. When the U.S. Army performed the experiments on the donor and his cells, the DNA acted as if it were still connected to the person having the emotions. Even when the donor and his DNA were separated by distances of up to 350 miles, the results were the same, and the mystery remained, because our conventional explanations for why DNA would respond to its owner's emotions are invalid.

Most people would assume that some energy was being shared in this experiment. When we think of energy, we typically imagine it being generated in one place and then somehow transmitted or conveyed to another. Just as the image on our TV set or our favorite music on the radio is the result of energy being broadcast from point A to point B, we would expect some kind of force to travel from the donor to his DNA. For a transfer to happen, however, it takes time to get from one location to the next. While this interval might not be much, maybe just a nanosecond, some amount of time must pass for a conventional energy to move from one point to another.

The key in the experiment, however, was that an atomic clock (accurate to one second in one million years) showed that no such time elapsed. The effect was simultaneous because no exchange was necessary. On the quantum level, the donor and the DNA were both part of the same pattern, and the information from either one was already present with the other: They were already connected. The energy from the donor's emotions never traveled *anywhere,* because it was already *everywhere.*

Any change that we wish to see in our world—from healing and safety for our loved ones to peace in the Middle East or any of the 60-plus nations now engaged in armed conflict—doesn't have to be sent from our hearts and minds to the places where it's needed. It's not necessary to "send" anything anywhere. Once our prayers are inside of us, they're already everywhere.

Key 14: The universally connected hologram of consciousness promises that the instant we create our good wishes and prayers, they are already received at their destination.

The implications of this principle are vast and deep. To really know what it means in our lives, however, we need to examine the last piece of how the hologram works: the power to create change within it. If everything is really connected and already everywhere all the time, then what happens when we change something in one part of the hologram? Once again, the answer may surprise you.

A CHANGE ANYWHERE MEANS A CHANGE EVERYWHERE

In the movie *Contact*, there are scenes that flash back to the childhood of the lead character and show the influence that her father had in her life before his sudden death. Offering his support for the ambitious way she approached her goals, he often commented that the great things in his daughter's future would be accomplished in small steps.

Not only is this great advice for all parents to pass along to their children, it appears to be precisely the way the hologram of consciousness and life works. When we make a little change here and another one there, suddenly *everything* seems to change. In fact, a small alteration in one place can permanently shift an entire paradigm.

Visionary and philosopher Ervin Laszlo describes the reason why this is so: "All that happens in one place happens also in other places; all that happened at one time happens also at times after that. Nothing is 'local,' limited to where and when it is happening."[7] As the great spiritual teachers such as Mahatma Gandhi and Mother Teresa demonstrated so eloquently, the nonlocal holographic principle is an immense force—a "David" to the "Goliath" of change in the quantum world.

Just as a hologram contains the original image in all of its many parts, any change made to just one of those segments becomes reflected everywhere throughout the pattern. What a powerful relationship! A single change in one place can make a difference everywhere! Perhaps the best example of how little modifications can affect an entire system can be seen in something that we're all familiar with: the DNA of our bodies.

Watching any movie based on modern crime-scene investigation, we learn quickly that the identity of the perpetrator can be detected from traces of him or her left at the place where the crime was committed. If the investigators can identify any part of a person's body or anything that comes from it—from a splatter of blood or a broken strand of hair to stains of semen or even torn fingernails—then they can identify someone. And it makes no difference where in the body the DNA comes from because of the holographic principle—all parts mirror the whole. Each piece of DNA exactly resembles the others (barring mutations).

It's estimated that the average human has between 50 and 100 trillion cells in his or her body. Each of those cells holds 23 pairs of chromosomes that contain an individual's DNA (life code). When we do the math, this means that people carry somewhere between 2,300 trillion and 4,600 trillion copies of DNA in their bodies. Just imagine how long it would take to make a change in someone's DNA if we attempted to update each copy, one cell at a time. But when DNA does modify the blueprint of a species, it doesn't have to do so in a linear fashion, one strand at time. Because of the holographic principle, when the DNA is altered, that change is reflected throughout the whole.

Key 15: Through the hologram of consciousness, a little change in our lives is mirrored everywhere in our world.

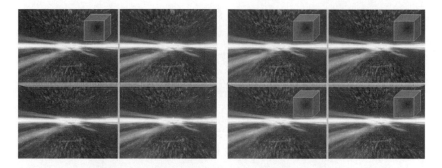

Figure 10. In a hologram, every part of "something" reflects every other part, and change is mirrored throughout the whole. Even if we divide the universe into four smaller fragments, for example, every piece is a mirror of the entire universe. A change in one place (indicated by the lightened section) is reflected in every mirror.

You're probably asking yourself, *Why is this important in my life?* While this is an obvious question, the answer may be less so. The subtle power of the hologram is that it offers us the leverage to make a tremendous change on a large scale by altering a pattern in only one place. Understanding the holographic principle is important because it appears to describe precisely the way we work. From the DNA of our bodies to the atomic structure of the world around us to how memory and consciousness work, we appear to be holograms of a greater existence that we're only beginning to understand.

HOLOGRAPHIC BRAINS IN A HOLOGRAPHIC UNIVERSE

I remember watching a documentary in the 1970s on the human brain in which surgeons were preparing to relieve pressure deep within the tissue of a man's brain caused by the trauma of an accident. While he was wide-awake and conscious, portions of his exposed brain were stimulated with electrical probes to see what part of the body those segments were related to. When an electrode was touched to one place, for example, the patient would "see" a burst of color, and that location would be noted as a visual center.

Aside from the bizarre experience of seeing a living brain exposed to the bright lights of the operating room, what made this particular film so interesting was the way the man's brain was working. When certain sites were electrically stimulated and produced his experience of seeing color, for example, those places didn't seem to correspond to the ones that are traditionally associated with vision. It was as if portions of his brain had somehow learned to "see" in a way that we would normally expect to find in another part of the brain.

The revolutionary work of neuroscientist Karl Pribram has also found that cerebral functions are more global than was once postulated. Prior to Pribram's work, it was believed that our brains work like amazing biological computers that store particular kinds of information in precise places. In this mechanical model of memory, there was a one-to-one correspondence between certain types of memory and the locations where they were stored. The problem was that localized memory wasn't what was found in laboratory experiments.

In much the same way that the documentary showed places in the man's brain that "knew" the function of other areas, experiments demonstrated that animals retained memories and continued their lives even though the parts of their brains that were believed to hold these functions were removed. In other words, it appeared that there wasn't a direct correspondence between the memories and a physical place in the brain. It was obvious that the mechanical view of brains and memory wasn't the answer— something else strange and wonderful must be happening.

In the early 1970s, Pribram pioneered a powerful new model to explain the evidence from the experiments. He began to think of the brain and memories within it as working like holograms. One of the keys that confirmed Pribram was on the right track was the laboratory validation of the way we mentally process information. He drew upon earlier research to test his hypothesis. In the 1940s, scientist Dennis Gabor used a complex set of equations known as

Fourier transforms (named after their discoverer, Joseph Fourier) to create the first holograms, work for which he was awarded a Nobel Prize in 1971. Pribram guessed that if the brain does in fact work like a hologram, distributing information throughout its soft circuits, then it should process information the same way Fourier's equations do.

Knowing that the brain's cells create electrical waves, Pribram was able test the patterns from the circuits using the Fourier transforms. Sure enough, his theory was accurate—the experiments proved that our brains process information in a way that's equivalent to the equations of a hologram.

Pribram clarified his model of the brain through a simple metaphor of holograms within holograms. In an interview, he stated, "The holograms within the visual system are . . . patch holograms."[8] These are smaller portions of a larger image. "The total image is composed much as it is in an insect eye that has hundreds of little lenses instead of one single big lens. . . . You get the total pattern all woven together as a unified piece by the time you experience it."[9]

Interestingly, while Pribram and David Bohm (whose ideas were discussed in the Introduction) began their work independently, both were using the same explanation to describe the results of their experiments. They were each applying the holographic model to make sense of life. Bohm, as a quantum physicist, was looking at the universe as a hologram. Pribram, as a neuroscientist, was studying the brain as a holographic processor, with our minds performing holographic processes. When the two theories are combined, what results is nothing less than a paradigm-shattering possibility.

That possibility suggests that we are part of a much greater system of many realities, within realities, within other realities. In this system, our world could be considered a shadow or a projection of events that are happening in a deeper, underlying reality. What we see as our universe is really us—our individual and collective minds—transforming the possibilities of the deeper realms into physical reality. This radically new way of viewing ourselves and the universe gives nothing less than direct access to every possibility that we could ever wish (or pray) for, dream, or imagine.

In his studies, Pribram offers a reason for precisely such possibilities. Through the holographic model of the brain interacting with the universe, he says that the functioning of our brain allows for experiences that transcend time and space. Within the context of this holographic model, all things become possible. The key to experiencing the power of these potential outcomes is that we must think of ourselves in this new way. And when we do, something wonderful begins to happen: We're changed.

It's impossible for us to "kind of" or "sort of" see ourselves as empowered beings in a universe of possibilities—we either do or we don't. And that's precisely the focus of this book. We can think of ourselves differently only when we have a reason to do so. The concept of the Divine Matrix as a universally connected hologram promises us that we're limited only by our beliefs.

As the ancient spiritual traditions suggest, the invisible walls of our deepest beliefs can become our greatest prison. Yet they also remind us that it's our beliefs that can become our greatest source of freedom. As different as the world's wisdom traditions may be from one another, they all bring us to the same conclusion: *The opportunity to be imprisoned or free is ours, and we're the only ones who can make the choice.*

THE POWER OF A MUSTARD SEED

The pioneering work of Karl Pribram and the studies by other researchers who have followed show that our brains function as holographic information processors. If this is true for us as individuals, then it makes sense that our collective mind and consciousness may work this way as well. Today more than six billion humans (and minds) inhabit the planet. Within the container of the Divine Matrix, each individual's mind is part of a larger single awareness.

Regardless of how different they may appear from one another, every mind contains the pattern of the whole consciousness. And through that link, we each have direct access to the entire pattern. In other words, we all have the power to change the hologram of our world. While for some people this is an unconventional way to think about who we are, for others it's perfectly aligned with their beliefs and experiences.

Scientific studies support these principles and have found that when people *within* a group share a common experience of consciousness, the effects can be detected *beyond* the group itself and even outside the building where the individuals are meeting. Clearly, inner experiences are being carried through some subtle conduit in a way that's not restricted by the so-called laws of physics or limited to the immediate surroundings. One example of this phenomenon is evident in the effect that Transcendental Meditation (TM) can have upon large populations.

In 1972, 24 cities in the U.S. with populations over 10,000 experienced meaningful changes in their communities when as few as one percent (100 people) participated in the studies. Those involved used specific meditation techniques to create the inner experiences of peace that were mirrored in the world around them. This is called the "Maharishi Effect" in honor of Maharishi Mahesh Yogi, who stated that when one percent of a population practiced the methods of meditation that he offered, there would be a reduction in violence and crime for that population.

These and similar studies led to a landmark project, "International Peace Project in the Middle East," published in the *Journal of Conflict Resolution* in 1988.[10] During the Israeli-Lebanese war of the early 1980s, practitioners were trained in precise techniques of TM to create peace in their bodies, rather than simply thinking about it in their minds or praying for it to occur.

On specific days of the month, at specific times each day, these people were positioned within the war-torn areas of the Middle East. During the window of time that they were at peace, terrorist incidents, crimes against people, emergency-room visits, and traffic accidents all declined in number. When the participants stopped their practice, the statistics reversed. These studies confirmed the earlier findings: When a small percentage of the population achieved peace within themselves, that peace was reflected in the world around them.

The results took into account the days of the week, holidays, and even lunar cycles; and they were so consistent that the researchers were able to identify the minimum number of people needed to experience inner peace before it's mirrored in the surrounding world: the square root of one percent of the population. This represents only the base number required for the effect to begin— the more people participate, the more pronounced the outcome. While we may not fully understand all the reasons why the effects are present, the correlations and results demonstrate that they are there. We can apply this principle in our lives for any group of people, regardless of whether it's a small community, a church congregation, a large city, or the entire planet. To determine how many people are needed to work together for peace and healing in that group, the formula suggests the following:

1. Determine the total number of people present.

2. Calculate one percent of that total number (multiply the total from step 1 by .01).

3. Calculate the square root of the one percent (enter the number from step 2, and press the √ function on your calculator).

This formula produces numbers that are smaller than we might expect. For example, in a city of a million people, the total is about 100. In a world of 6 billion people, it's only about 8,000. And this calculation represents only the minimum needed to begin the process. The more people are involved, the faster the effect is created.

While these and similar studies obviously deserve more exploration, they show there's an effect that's beyond chance.

> **Key 16:** The minimum number of people required to "jump-start" a change in consciousness is the $\sqrt{1\%}$ of a population.

Perhaps this is the reason why so many wisdom traditions emphasize the importance of each individual to the whole. In one of the best-known parables of the power of belief, Jesus used the holographic principle to illustrate how just a little faith is all that's required to open the door to a greater possibility. "In truth," he said, "if your faith is the size of a mustard seed you will say to this mountain, 'Move from here to there' and it will move; nothing will be impossible for you."[11] We'll explore the implications of just what this means in the following section. Before we do, however, a brief clarification of what's meant by "faith" is appropriate here.

The word *faith* itself can sometimes carry a bit of an emotional charge, as it's often associated with a belief that has no apparent foundation or basis to support it. We commonly hear this referred to as "blind faith." My sense is that there really is no such thing as absolutely blind faith. Somewhere deep inside of us, all our beliefs come from the feeling of a deeper connection between the things that "are" and the things that can be. While we may not always be conscious of this or be able to state *why* we think that something is so, our beliefs are true for us. And that truth is the foundation of faith.

There is a kind of faith, however, that's actually based in a very solid foundation of leading-edge science, supported by the discoveries of quantum physics. In Chapter 3, we briefly discussed the possible reasons why the physical world is changed by simply observing it. All of the explanations that followed acknowledged the coexistence of many realities within a cosmic soup of possibilities. As the experiments showed, it's the act of our watching something—that is, *conscious observation*—that locks one of those possibilities into place as *our* reality. In other words, *the expectation or belief that we have while we're observing* is the ingredient in the soup that "chooses" which possibility becomes our "real" experience.

With this in mind, the faith in Jesus's statement is more than simply saying the words to represent that the mountain has moved. In a parable that's nearly 2,000 years old, we're taught a powerful language with which to choose reality from the infinite possibilities that already exist. As Neville states so clearly in his description of faith, through the act of "persisting in the assumption that your desire is already fulfilled . . . your world inevitably conforms to your assumption."[12] In the example of the mountain, when we truly know that it's already moved, our faith/belief/assumption that it's happened is the energy that jolts that possibility into our reality. In the quantum realm of all possibilities, the mountain has no choice—it must move.

The following example illustrates just how simple and natural this kind of faith and belief can be. It also opens the door to countless possibilities for how a small shift in our viewpoint can create a huge difference in our world.

A few years ago, I had the opportunity to witness the biological equivalent of "moving the mountain." In this case, the "mountain" was a life-threatening tumor inside the bladder of a middle-aged woman. Western doctors had diagnosed the mass as malignant and believed that it was inoperable. In the makeshift classroom of our hotel ballroom, the group I was part of was shown a film created by our instructor when he had been present for the miraculous healing of the growth in a hospital without medicine in Beijing, China.[13]

The clinic was one of the many in the region that routinely use nontraditional methods of treatment with tremendous success. After exchanging greetings and the formalities of introductions, we were prepared for what we were about to see. The instructor emphasized that the purpose of the film was to show us that the power to heal is something that lives within each of us. It was *not* an advertisement for the clinic or an invitation for everyone with a life-threatening condition to make a mad dash to Beijing. What we were about to witness could be accomplished right there in our classroom or at home in our living rooms. The key to healing, he said, is the ability to focus emotion and energy in our bodies or that of a loved one (with the person's permission) in a noninvasive and compassionate way.

The woman in the film had come to the clinic without medicine as a last resort because all else had failed. The facility emphasizes personal responsibility in our health and provides new and life-affirming ways of living, rather than simply "fixing" people and sending them home. These protocols include new eating habits, gentle forms of movement to stimulate the life force (chi) within the body, and novel methods of breathing. By following these simple changes in lifestyle, the client's body is strengthened for the healing that's possible. Following these procedures, at some point it makes sense for clinic patients to undergo the treatment that was recorded on the video.

As the handheld film began, we could see the woman with the tumor lying on what appeared to be a hospital gurney. She was awake, fully conscious, and had been given no sedative or anesthetic. Three practitioners in white lab coats stood behind her while an ultrasound technician was seated in front of her, holding the wand that would be used to create a sonogram to view the mass inside of her body. We were told that the image wouldn't be time-lapsed in the way that nature programs show the days-long process of a rosebud opening condensed into seconds. Our film would be in real time so that we could see the true effect of the practitioners' healing.

The film was short, lasting less than four minutes. Within that time span, we all saw something that's considered a miracle by the standards of Western medicine. Yet within the holographic context of the Divine Matrix, it's something that makes perfect sense. The practitioners had agreed upon a word that would reinforce for them a special quality of feeling inside their bodies. Reminding us of Neville's instruction to "make your future dream a present fact . . . by assuming the feeling of your wish fulfilled," the practitioners' emotion was simply one of the woman already healed.[14] Although they knew that the tumor had existed in the moments leading up to the process, they also acknowledged that its presence was only one possibility out of the many that exist. On that day, they enacted the code that calls for another possibility. And they did so in the language that the Matrix recognizes and responds to—that of human emotion directing energy (see Chapter 3).

Watching the practitioners, we heard them repeat the words of a mantra of sorts, which loosely translates into the English words "already done, already done." At first it seemed that nothing was happening. Suddenly, the tumor began to quiver in and out of view, as if it were teetering between realities. The room was absolutely silent as we watched the screen in awe. Within seconds, it faded and then completely vanished from the screen . . . it was gone. Everything else was there, just as it had been seconds before—everything, that is, except the tumor that had threatened the woman's life. The room looked the same. The practitioners and the technician were present, and nothing "spooky" seemed to have happened anywhere else; just the condition that had previously endangered the woman's life had disappeared.

I remember thinking of the ancient admonition that with a little faith, mountains could be moved. I also recall pondering that before that moment, I'd always believed that the moving of mountains was a metaphor—now I knew that it was a literal fact. Using the formula of the square root of one percent, the population of the clinic had proven that consciousness can directly affect our reality.

There were a total of six people in the room while the healing happened (three practitioners, the technician, the camera operator, and the woman with the condition). Applying the formula, the square root of one percent of that room's population was only .244 of a person! With the requirement of less than one person's belief in the absolute knowing that the healing had already happened, the physical reality of the woman's body changed.

Although the number in this case was small, the formula still held true. As noted before, that total is the *minimum* needed to jump-start a new reality. In all probability, 100 percent of the people in the room experienced the feeling of her healing, and it took two minutes and 40 seconds for her body to mirror their reality.

With permission, I have since shown this film to many audiences—including medical personnel—throughout the world. The reactions vary and are predictable. Once the healing happens, there's generally a brief silence as the viewers register in their hearts and minds what they've just seen with their eyes. The silence gives way to sighs of joy, laughter, and even applause. For some people, watching the film is a confirmation of what they already believe to be true. Even faith is bolstered by the validation of really seeing something that's possible.

For others who are more skeptical, the question is typically: "If this is real, why don't we know about this?" My answer is: "Now you do!" "How long does the healing effect last?" is the next query. The studies have shown a 95 percent success rate after five years for clients who continue the life-affirming changes in nutrition, breath, and movement learned in the clinic.

After a gasp coming from somewhere between the desire to believe and frustration that so many people couldn't be helped by modern techniques, I usually hear something along the lines of: "This is too simple . . . it just can't be that easy!"

My response is: "Why would we expect anything less?" In the holographic world of the Divine Matrix, all things are possible, and we choose our possibilities.

Believing that we are "here" and the possibilities are "out there," however, sometimes gives us the feeling that they're inaccessible. The same rules that describe *how* the Divine Matrix works also tell us that in the deeper reality, what we typically think of as "somewhere else" is really already "here," and vice versa. It's all about the way we see ourselves in the field of possibilities.

Knowing that everything from the most horrible suffering to the most joyous ecstasy—and all possibilities in between—already exist, we find that it makes perfect sense that we have the power to collapse the intervening space and bring those possibilities into our lives. And we do . . . through the silent language of imagination, dreams, and belief.

CHAPTER FIVE

WHEN HERE IS THERE AND THEN IS NOW:
JUMPING TIME AND SPACE IN THE MATRIX

> *"Time is not at all what it
> seems. It does not flow in only
> one direction, and the future exists
> simultaneously with the past."*
> — Albert Einstein (1879–1955),
> physicist
>
> *"Time is what prevents everything
> from happening at once."*
> — John Wheeler (1911–), physicist

"Time is / Too Slow for those who Wait, / Too Swift for those who Fear, / Too Long for those who grieve, / Too Short for those who Rejoice, / But for those who Love, / Time is not." With these words, poet Henry Van Dyke reminds us of our ironic relationship with time.

Time is perhaps the most elusive of all human experiences. We can't capture or photograph it. Contrary to what daylight saving would seem to imply, it's impossible to gather it in one place only to use it later in another. When we do attempt to describe the meaning of time in our lives, we're left using words that gauge it in a relative sense. We say that something happened *then* in the past, it's happening *now* in the present, or it will happen *at some point* in the future. The only way we can describe time is through the things that happen *within* it.

As mysterious as time is, it's been the focus of human attention for thousands of years. For countless centuries, we've worked to devise and refine systems of keeping track of time as cycles and as cycles within cycles for very good reason. For instance, to know when to plant the crops that will sustain an entire civilization, it's important to be aware of how many days, lunar cycles, and eclipses have passed since the last planting. Ancient systems of timekeeping maintain a precise record of this. The Mayan calendar, for example, calculates cycles of time that began in 3113 B.C. (more than 5,000 years ago), while the Hindu system of yugas tracks the progression of creation cycles that began more than 4 million years ago!

Until the 20th century, in the Western world time was typically thought of in a poetic sense, as an artifact of human experience. Philosopher Jean-Paul Sartre described our relationship to time as "a special kind of separation: a division that reunites." But that poetic view changed in 1905 when Einstein posited his theory of relativity. Before relativity, time was believed to be its own experience, distinct from the three dimensions of height, length, and width that define space. In his theory, however, Einstein proposed that space and time are intimately entwined and can't be separated. It is space-time together, he said, that forms a realm beyond our familiar three-dimensional experience: the fourth dimension. Suddenly, time became more than a casual philosophical concept . . . it was a force to be reckoned with.

In words that brought a new meaning to our perception of time, Einstein described its mysterious nature by simply stating the obvious: "The distinction between past, present, and future is only a stubbornly persistent illusion."[1] With this powerful assertion, Einstein forever changed the way we think of our relationship to time. Consider the implications . . . if the past and the future are present in this moment, can we communicate with them? Can we travel in time?

Even before Einstein's bold statement, the possibilities that these questions posed intrigued scientists, mystics, and writers. From hidden temples in Egypt dedicated to the experience of time to the thrill of H. G. Wells's classic 1895 novel *The Time Machine,* the prospect of having an ability to somehow hitch a ride on the flow of time has captured our imaginations and filled our dreams. Our fascination with it is as old as our existence, and our questions about it seem endless.

Is time real? Does it exist without us? Is there something about consciousness that gives time its meaning? If so, do we have the power or the right to interrupt its forward flow long enough to glimpse the future . . . or perhaps visit or communicate with people in the past? Can we contact other realms and even other worlds with which we share the present?

In light of accounts such as the one in the following section, the boundary between "here" and "there" becomes less clear, inviting us to reconsider just what time really means in our lives.

A MESSAGE FROM BEYOND TIME

In the powerful book *Small Miracles: Extraordinary Coincidences from Everyday Life,* Yitta Halberstam and Judith Leventhal share an amazing story of the power of forgiveness.[2] While I've done my best to capture the essence of this awe-inspiring account, I encourage you to experience it in its entirety in the original text. What makes this story so interesting, and the reason I offer it here, is that in this case forgiveness is so powerful that it transcends time.

> *The news of his father's death came as a shock to Joey. They hadn't spoken since he'd turned 19 and had questioned his family's traditional Jewish beliefs. To Joey's father, there could be no greater disgrace than to doubt such a time-honored philosophy. He threatened to end their relationship unless his son accepted his roots and stopped his questioning. Joey found that he couldn't meet his dad's demands, so he left home to explore the world. He and his father never spoke again.*
>
> *It was in a small café in India that a friend found Joey and shared the news of Joey's father's death. This was the first that Joey knew of his passing. He immediately returned home and began to explore his Jewish heritage. Deeply moved by new*

insights into his background and his father, Joey found himself making plans for a personal pilgrimage to the land where the roots of his family's traditions began: He was on his way to Israel.

This is where the story takes a deep, mystical turn and offers us insight into the power of the Divine Matrix.

Joey found himself at the Wailing Wall in Jerusalem, the portion of an ancient temple enclosure that remained following the temple's destruction nearly 2,000 years ago. It's here that Orthodox Jews go to worship each day, repeating the words of the same prayers that have been spoken for centuries.

Joey had written a note to his father, declaring his love and asking forgiveness for the pain that he had caused his family. Following the custom, he'd planned to leave his note in one of the many cracks and crevices that were formed when the original mortar fell away from between the stones. It was when Joey found just the right place to leave his note that something amazing happened—something that has no rational explanation in the eyes of traditional Western science.

As Joey put his note in the wall, another paper suddenly fell from between the stones, landing at his feet. It was a prayer that someone else had written and placed in the wall weeks or possibly even months before. As Joey reached for the rolled-up paper, an odd feeling came over him.

When Joey opened the note and began to read its contents, he recognized the handwriting—it was his father's! The note that Joey held was one that his dad had written and left in the wall before his death. In it, he had declared his love for his son and asked God for forgiveness. At some time in the not-too-distant past, Joey's father had traveled to the very spot where Joey found himself at that moment. In an ironic twist of synchronicity, his father had placed his prayer in that same precise location within the wall, where it had remained until Joey walked by.

What a powerful story! How could such an extraordinary thing have happened? Obviously, there must be some kind of communication happening between realities and worlds. Joey lives in the realm of the present that we call "our world." Although his father was no longer alive, Judaism believes that he still exists in another realm, the *ha-shamayim,* or heaven, which lies beyond our world. Both realms are thought to coexist in the present and to be in communication with one another.

While the mechanics of precisely *how* the message from Joey's dad reached him may remain a mystery, one thing is certain: For Joey to receive an indication that his father is still in touch with him, there must be something that connects both of them, a medium that provides the container for both realms of experience. The Divine Matrix is that medium—it fits the description of the place the ancients called heaven: the home of the soul that's the container for the past, present, and future.

Through the bridge of the Divine Matrix, something beautiful and precious transpired between Joey and his father. Transcending time, space, and (in this story) even life and death, a communication occurred that brought healing and closure between a father and his son. We must look even deeper into our relationship with the space that creates *here* and *there* and the time that allows for *then* and *now* to understand how this happened and why.

WHEN HERE IS THERE

If our universe and everything in it are truly held within the container of the Divine Matrix, as the experiments suggest, then we may soon find ourselves redefining our ideas of space as well as time. We could even discover that the distances that seem to cut us off from one another and our loved ones only separate our bodies. As we saw in the story of Joey and his father, something within us isn't bound by distance or limited by the traditional laws of physics.

While these possibilities may sound like the stuff of science fiction, they're also the subjects of serious scientific investigation—so serious, in fact, that during the last years of the Cold War, both the U.S. and the former Soviet Union devoted tremendous amounts of money and research to understanding precisely how real the Matrix that connects everything actually is. Specifically, the superpowers wanted to know if it's possible to navigate great distances through the Matrix by using the inner sight of the mind—the psychic abilities of a certain kind of telepathy known as *remote viewing.* The results might sound surprisingly similar to some popular movies of recent years and may very well be the precise basis of their plots. The experiments also make the already blurred line between fact and fiction fuzzier than ever.

In 1970, the U.S. officially began investigating the possibility of using psychic methods to "surf" the Matrix and see into distant lands and enemy targets. It was then that the CIA funded the early experiments using psychically sensitive people such as empaths (individuals who have the ability to sense the experiences of others without the need for verbal or visual cues) to focus their minds on classified locations.[3] Once they did so, they were trained to describe what they found with increasingly greater detail. Given the acronym SCANATE, for "scan by coordinate," this program was one of the precursors that led to the now-famous studies at the Stanford Research Institute (SRI) on remote viewing.

Although in some respects remote viewing may seem a little "out there," it's actually based on sound quantum principles, some of which have already been explored in this book. Even the experts acknowledge that no one knows precisely how remote viewing works. In general, its success is attributed to the idea from quantum physics that while things may look solid and separate to us, they exist and are connected to everything else as a universal field of energy. For example, while we may hold a beautiful seashell in our hand, from a quantum perspective, there's an energetic part of the shell that's everywhere. Because our shell exists beyond the *local* place where we hold it in our hand, it is said to be "nonlocal."

A growing number of scientists accept the experimental evidence that the universe, planet, and even our bodies are nonlocal. We are everywhere already and always. As Russell Targ stated in Chapter 4, even though we may be physically separated from one another, we can still be in instantaneous communication—and that's what remote viewing is all about.

In effect, viewers in the SCANATE program were taught how to have a waking, or "lucid," dream. In their altered state, they gave their consciousness the freedom to focus on precise locations. These sites could be in another room of the same building or on the other side of the world. Clarifying the connectedness of our universe in the quantum realm, Targ states, "It's no harder to describe what's happening in the far reaches of the Soviet Union than it is to describe what's happening across the street."[4] The trainees received as many as three years of instruction before they were deployed on secret missions.

The details of the U.S. military's remote-viewing projects, which have been made available to the general public only recently, describe at least two kinds of sessions. The first, called coordinate remote viewing, involves viewers' descriptions of what they find at specific geographic coordinates, as identified by latitude and longitude. The second, called extended remote viewing, is based on a series of relaxation and meditative techniques.

Although the specifics may vary by method, in general, remote-viewing procedures begin with viewers entering a mild state of relaxation, since it's in this state that they appear to be more open to receiving sensory impressions of distant locations. During the sessions, another person is generally involved as a guide whose role is to help the viewer by prompting him or her to look at specific details. Through a series of protocols that allow the viewer to distinguish which impressions are important for the particular "mission," the person is able to describe what he or she sees with increasingly deeper levels of detail. The prompting of the guide seems to separate this form of controlled remote viewing from the lucid dreaming that often happens spontaneously during sleep.

The implications for secrecy were immense and opened the door to a new era of intelligence gathering with fewer risks to people on the ground—fewer risks, that is, until the remote-viewing programs were shut down in the mid-1990s. With intriguing code names such as Project Stargate, the last one was "officially" terminated in 1995. Although the process was considered by some to be a "fringe" science and even discounted altogether by military skeptics, a number of remote-viewing sessions were validated through successes that couldn't be attributed to coincidence. Some may have even saved lives.

During the first Gulf War in 1991, remote viewers were asked to search for enemy missile locations hidden in the deserts of western Iraq.[5] The project successfully pinpointed specific missile sites and eliminated other areas from consideration. The advantages of such a psychic search are obvious. By narrowing down the possible locations where the weapons could be, everything from time to fuel and money was saved. The greatest benefit, however, was to the lives of the troops themselves. The remote search for deadly missiles reduced the risk to soldiers who traditionally would have had to perform such a mission on the ground.

The reason why I mention these projects and techniques here is because they successfully demonstrate two things that are key in our understanding of the Divine Matrix. First, they are yet another indication that the Matrix exists. For a part of us to travel to distant locations and see the details of things that are very real without ever leaving the chair we're sitting in, there must be something for our awareness to travel through. My main point here is that a viewer has access to the destination, regardless of where it is. Second, the very nature of the energy that makes remote viewing possible shows the holographic connectedness that appears to be a part of our identity. In the presence of evidence of the Divine Matrix, the old ideas of who we are and how we function in space-time begin to break down.

THE LANGUAGE THAT MIRRORS REALITY

While Western science is only beginning to understand what our relationship to time and space mean within the context of connectedness, our indigenous ancestors were already well aware of these relationships. When linguist Benjamin Lee Whorf explored the language of the Hopi, for example, he found that their words directly reflected their view of the universe. And their idea of who we are as humans is very different from the way we typically think of ourselves—they saw the world as a single entity with everything in it connected at the source.

In his groundbreaking book *Language, Thought, and Reality,* Whorf summarized the Hopi worldview: "In [the] Hopi view, time disappears and space is altered, so that it is no longer the homogeneous and instantaneous timeless space of our supposed intuition or of classical Newtonian mechanics."[6] In other words, the Hopi simply don't think of time, space, distance, and reality in the way we do. In their eyes, we live in a universe where everything is alive, connected, and happening "now." And their language mirrors this perspective.

For example, when we look to the ocean and see a wave, we might say, "Look at that wave." But we know that in reality it doesn't exist alone; it's only there because of other waves. "[W]ithout the projection of language," says Whorf, "no one ever saw a single wave."[7] What we see is a "surface in everchanging undulating motions." In the language of the Hopi, however, speakers would say that the ocean is "waving" to describe the present action of the water. More precisely, according to Whorf, "Hopi say *walalata,* meaning 'plural waving occurs,' and can call attention to one place in the waving just as we can."[8] In this way, although it may sound odd to us, they are actually more accurate in how they describe the world.

In a similar vein, the concept of time as we tend to think of it takes on a brand-new meaning in the traditional beliefs of the Hopi. Whorf's studies led him to discover that the "manifested comprises all that is or has been accessible to the senses, the historical physical universe . . . with no attempt to distinguish between present and past, but excluding everything that we call future."⁹ In other words, the Hopi use the same words to identify only what "is" or has already happened. From the previous discussions of quantum possibilities, this view of time and language makes perfect sense. The Hopi are describing the possibilities that have been chosen, while leaving the future open.

From the implications of the Hopi language to the proven examples of remote viewing, our relationship to space and time obviously has more to it than we have traditionally acknowledged. The essence of the new physics suggests that space-time cannot be separated. So if we rethink what distance means to us within the Divine Matrix, then it's clear that we must reconsider our relationship to time as well. This is where the possibilities get really interesting.

WHEN THEN IS NOW

In addition to helping our kids get to soccer practice while the rest of the team is still on the field and assuring that we're at the airport to meet our departing flight, what *is* time, really? Are the seconds between the minutes that make up our day all that keeps things from running together, as stated in John Wheeler's quote at the beginning of this chapter? Does time exist if no one knows about it?

Perhaps an even deeper question is whether or not the things that happen in time are "fixed." Are the events of the universe already inscribed in a timeline that's simply playing out as our lives? Or is time somehow malleable? And if so, are the events within it changeable?

Conventional thinking suggests that time only moves in one direction—forward—and what's already happened is in fact etched into the fabric of time and space. Experimental evidence, however, indicates that our ideas of the past and present may not be quite so neat and tidy. Not only does it appear that time moves in two directions, as Einstein posited, but it also seems as if the choices of today might actually change what took place yesterday. In 1983, an experiment was designed to test just such possibilities. The results run absolutely counter to the way we've been led to think about time, and the implications are mind-boggling.

For this investigation, physicist John Wheeler proposed using a variation of the famous double-slit experiment to test the effects of the present on the past. Here's a brief summary of the original experiment described in Chapter 2.

A quantum particle (a photon) was fired at a target that could detect how it arrived—either as a particle of matter or as a wave of energy. Before reaching the target, however, it had to pass through the opening in a barrier. The mystery was that the photon somehow "knew" when the barrier had one hole and when it had two.

In the presence of a single opening, the particle traveled and arrived at its destination just the way it began its journey: as a particle. However, in the presence of two holes, while it started off the experiment as a particle, it moved as a wave of energy through both openings at the same time and acted like a wave at its destination.

The outcome: It was determined that since the scientists performing the experiment were the only ones who knew about the openings in the barrier, their knowledge somehow influenced how the photon behaved.

Wheeler's variation of this experiment included one key difference designed to test his ideas of past and present. He changed the experiment so that the photon is only observed *after* it has already passed through the barrier, yet *before* it gets to its destination. In other words, it's *already on its way* to the target when the decision is made as to how it will be viewed.

He designed two very different ways to know that the photon has reached its target: One uses a lens to "see" it visually as a particle, while the other uses a screen that senses it as a wave. This is important, since the previous experiments showed that the photons acted the way they were expected to depending upon how they were observed—that is, they were particles when measured as particles and waves when measured as waves.

So in this experiment, if the observer chose to see the photon as a particle, the lens would be in place and the photon would travel through one slit only. If the observer chose to view it as a wave, the screen would remain in place and the photon would pass through both slits as a wave. Here's the clincher: The decision was made *after* the experiment was under way (the present), yet it determined how the particle behaved when the experiment began (the past). Wheeler named this test the delayed-choice experiment.

Based on this kind of investigation, it seems as though time as we know it in *our* world (the level of the physical) has no effect on the *quantum* realm (the level of energy). If a later choice determines how something happens in the past, Wheeler proposes that he then "may choose to know a property after the event should have already taken place."[10] The implications of what he's saying open the door to a powerful possibility for our relationship with time. Wheeler is suggesting that the choices we make today may, in fact, directly affect things that have already happened in the past. And if that's the case, it could change everything!

So, is it true? Do the decisions that we make right now influence, or even determine, what's already occurred? While we've all heard from the great sages that we have the power to transcend our deepest hurts, does that ability extend to rewriting the past events that led to them? When we even ask such a question, it's difficult not to think of how messy things became when the lead character in the movie *Back to the Future,* Marty McFly (portrayed by Michael J. Fox), had the opportunity to do so. Imagine the possibilities, however, if we could learn from the suffering of the last century's great wars, for instance, or the painful divorce that we've just completed and make choices today that would prevent these things from happening. If we could, it would be the equivalent of a great *quantum eraser* allowing us to change the course of events that have brought us to our pain.

It is precisely this question that led to yet another variation of the double-slit experiment. Interestingly, this one is actually called the "quantum eraser" experiment. While its name sounds complicated, it's simple to explain and nothing less than paradigm shattering in its implications—so I'll cut to the chase.

The bottom line of what this experiment demonstrates is that the behavior of the particles when the experiment *begins* appears to be determined entirely by things that don't even happen until the experiment is finished.[11] In other words, the present has the power to change what's already occurred in the past. And this is the so-called quantum-eraser effect: Things that happen after the fact can change ("erase") the way the particles behave at an earlier point in time.

The question here is obvious: Does this effect apply only to quantum particles, or does it pertain to us as well?

Even though we're made of particles, maybe our consciousness is the glue that keeps us locked into the events—the wars, suffering, divorces, poverty, and disease—that we perceive as reality. Or perhaps something else is happening: It could be we *already* change our past as we learn from our mistakes, and we've been doing so all the time. Maybe it's so common for our choices to reverberate backward in time that this occurs without our knowing it or even giving it a second thought.

Perhaps the world that we see today, as tough as it sometimes appears, is the result of what we've already learned being reflected backward in time. It's certainly something to think about, and at the moment, it appears that research supports this possibility. If this is true and our world does in fact act like a cosmic feedback loop—with the lessons of the present changing the past—then just think about what that means! At the very least, it implies that the world we see today is the result of what we've already learned. And without our lessons, things could be much worse, couldn't they?

Regardless of whether or not we influence the past, it's clear that the choices we make now determine the present and future. And all three—past, present, and future—exist within the container of the Divine Matrix. It makes perfect sense that being part of the Matrix, we would be able to communicate with it in a way that's meaningful and useful in our lives. And according to scientific experiments, as well as our most cherished traditions, we do. The common denominator of the investigations in the previous chapters is twofold:

1. They show us that we're part of the Divine Matrix.

2. They demonstrate that human emotion (beliefs, expectations, and feelings) are the language that the Divine Matrix recognizes.

Interestingly, although perhaps coincidentally, these are the very experiences that were edited from Christian biblical texts and have been discouraged in Western culture. Today, however, all of that is changing. Men are being encouraged to honor their emotions, and women are exploring new ways to express the power that's such a natural part of their existence. It's clear that emotion, feeling, and belief are the language of the Divine Matrix, and there's a quality of emotion that allows us to experience the field of energy connecting the universe in ways that are powerful, healing, and natural.

The question now is: "If we're speaking to the Divine Matrix, how do we know when it answers us?" If our feelings, emotions, beliefs, and prayers are providing the blueprint for the quantum stuff of the universe, then what are our bodies, lives, and relationships telling us about our part of the conversation? To answer this, we must recognize the second half of our dialogue with the universe. So, how do we read the messages from the Divine Matrix?

PART III

MESSAGES FROM THE DIVINE MATRIX: LIVING, LOVING, AND HEALING IN QUANTUM AWARENESS

CHAPTER SIX

THE UNIVERSE IS TALKING TO US:
MESSAGES FROM THE MATRIX

> *"When love and hate
> are both absent, everything
> becomes clear and undisguised.
> Make the smallest distinction,
> however, and heaven
> and earth are set infinitely apart."*
> — Seng-ts'an, 6th-century philosopher
>
> *"We are the mirror
> as well as the face in it."*
> — Rumi, 13th-century poet

While we speak *to* the Divine Matrix through the language of feeling and belief, previous chapters also describe how the Matrix *answers us* through the events of our lives. In this dialogue, our deepest beliefs become the blueprint for everything that we experience. From the peace in our world to the healing in our bodies, from all our relationships and romances to the careers we pursue, our conversation with the world is constant and never ending. Because it doesn't stop, it's impossible for us to ever be passive observers on the sidelines of life . . . if we're conscious, by definition, we're creating.

Sometimes the dialogue is subtle and sometimes not. Regardless of the degree of subtlety, however, life in a reflected universe promises that from our challenges to our joys, the world is nothing more—or less—than the Matrix mirroring our deepest and truest beliefs. And this includes our intimate relationships. Although they present honest reflections, sometimes the mirrors we see of ourselves in other people can be the most difficult ones to accept. They can also be the fast track to our greatest healing.

OUR REFLECTED REALITY

In 1998, I had an experience in Tibet that offers a powerful metaphor for how the quantum "conversation" works. On the way into the capital city of Lhasa, our tour group was driving around a bend in the road that led to a small lake at the base of a cliff. The air was absolutely still, allowing the water to hold a perfect reflection of everything in the area.

From our vantage point, I could see the massive image of a beautifully carved Buddha mirrored in the water. Apparently, it was somewhere in the cliff overlooking the lake, although at that moment I couldn't see the carving itself—all I could see was the reflection. It was only when we came around the curve and the road leveled out that I saw with my eyes what I'd imagined was the source of the reflection. And there it was: Sculpted in high relief, the Buddha towered above the lake, liberated from the living rock as a silent witness to all who passed.

In that moment, the image in the lake became a metaphor for the visible world. As we were coming around the bend and I saw the Buddha in the water, the reflection was the only way I knew that a statue existed. Although I suspected that it was mirroring something physical, from my perspective, I simply couldn't see the object. In a similar way, the everyday world is said to be the reflection of a deeper reality carved into the fabric of the universe—a reality that we simply can't see from our place within it.

Figure 11. A reflecting Buddha carved in the cliff near Lhasa, Tibet.

Both ancient tradition and modern science suggest that what we see as the visible relationships of "life" are nothing more and nothing less than the reflection of things that are happening in another realm, a place that we can't perceive from our vantage point in the universe. And just as surely as I *knew* that the image in the water mirrored something that was real and solid, we can be sure that our lives are informing us about events occurring in another realm of existence. Just because we can't observe these events doesn't mean they aren't real. Ancient traditions suggest, in fact, that the unseen world is *more* real that the visible one! As Bohm said in the Introduction, we simply can't glimpse this "deeper reality" from where we are in space-time.

While we may not be able to see directly into this invisible realm, we do have some indication of what's happening there because we see its reflection in our everyday lives. From this perspective, our daily experiences serve as messages from these deeper realities—communication from *within* the Divine Matrix itself. And just as we must understand the words of any language to know its content, we must recognize the language of the Divine Matrix so that we can benefit from what it's telling us.

Sometimes the messages that come through are direct and can't be mistaken, while at other times, they're so subtle that we miss them altogether. Often, however, we may think that we're being shown one thing when, in fact, the messages are telling us something very different.

THINGS AREN'T ALWAYS WHAT THEY SEEM

"A sudden gust of wind hit me at that instant and made my eyes burn. I stared toward the area in question. There was absolutely nothing out of the ordinary.
'I can't see a thing,' I said.
'You just felt it,' he replied. [. . .]
'What? The wind?'
'Not just the wind,' he said sternly. 'It may seem to be wind to you, because wind is all you know.'"[1]

In this dialogue, the Yaqui Indian sorcerer Don Juan teaches his student Carlos Castenada about the subtle realities of the invisible world. In his book *Journey to Ixtlan,* Castenada, an anthropologist documenting the ways of the ancient shaman, learned very quickly that he couldn't trust the filters of his perceptions as he'd been conditioned to do in the past. The world, he found out, is alive on levels that are both seen and unseen.

For instance, Castenada had always been taught that when the bushes move beside you and you feel cool air brushing against your cheek, it's the wind that's moving. In the example above, Castenada's teacher reminds him that it only seems like the wind because that's what he knows. In reality, it could be the wind, or the feeling of a breeze against his face and flowing through his hair may be the energy of a spirit making itself known. Castenada rapidly discovered that such an experience would never be "just the wind" again.

Through our filters of perception, we do our best to fit our romances, friendships, finances, and health into the framework that past experiences have established. Although these boundaries may work, how well do they really serve us? How many times have we responded to life in a way that we learned from someone else, rather than based on what our own experiences have taught us? How often have we prevented ourselves from having greater abundance, deeper relationships, or more fulfilling jobs because an opportunity that crossed our path looked like a similar one from our past and we bolted in the opposite direction?

WE'RE TUNED TO OUR WORLD

Within the context of the Divine Matrix, we're part of each blade of grass, as well as every rock in every stream and river. We're part of each drop of rain and even the cool air that brushes against our faces when we walk out of our homes first thing in the morning.

If our link to everything in our world runs so deep, then it makes sense that we should see evidence of that connection in our lives every single day. Maybe we *do* in fact see precisely such evidence—and maybe we see it every day, only in ways that we may not always recognize or even notice.

We all know that the longer we're in the presence of the people, places, and things that surround us, the more we feel comfortable with them. For most of us, walking into the living room of our house, for example, certainly feels better than entering the "living room" of a hotel in another city. Even though the hotel may be newer and have all the latest fabrics, carpet, and upholstery, it just doesn't feel like "home." When we do experience something that way, our comfort comes from a fine-tuning of the subtle energy that brings us into balance with our world—we call that equilibrium *resonance*.

To some degree, we're in resonance with everything from our cars to our homes (and even the appliances that we rely on each day), which is why we affect other people, our surroundings, and our world simply by our presence. It should come as no surprise, then, that when something changes within us or the things around us, those changes will show up in our lives . . . and they do.

Sometimes these shifts come in ways that are subtle. For

example, I had an American-made car that had more than 300,000 miles on the original engine by the time I sold it in 1995. I'd always done my best to take care of my "old friend," a reliable vehicle that looked like new and carried me safely from the mountains of Colorado to the hills of Napa, California, and back to the high desert of northern New Mexico.

While my car always started and ran perfectly for me, it never failed to "break down" whenever I loaned it to someone else. Invariably, a new noise would begin in the engine, a warning light would appear on the dashboard, or it would simply stop running when another person with a different touch took over as the driver. And just as certainly, when I would slip back into the driver's seat and take it to the mechanic, the problem would just "heal itself," mysteriously disappearing.

While the mechanic assured me that "these things happen all the time," I'm sure that after a few such false alarms, he started to have second thoughts about me whenever he'd see my 300,000-mile Pontiac drive into his parking lot. While I can't prove it scientifically, I've talked to enough other people to know that this isn't an unusual experience. Things that are as familiar with us as we are with them simply seem to work better when they're in our presence. Sometimes, though, our resonance with the world appears to us in a way that's less subtle, with a message that's harder to miss—such as in the following example.

In the spring of 1990, I had left my career in the defense industry in Denver and was living temporarily in San Francisco. During the daytime I was developing seminars and writing my first book, while at night I was working as a counselor. Specifically, I was providing guidance in understanding the power of emotion in our lives and the role that it plays in our relationships. One of my first clients described a relationship that was a beautiful example of just how deep—and how literal—our resonance with the world can be.

She described the long-term relationship with the man in her life as the "never-ending date." For more than ten years, they'd been together in a relationship that appeared hopelessly stuck. Their conversations about marriage always seemed to end in bitter disagreements, yet they didn't do well apart from one another and wanted to share their lives together. One evening, my client described an experience of resonance that was so clear and powerful that it leaves little doubt that such a connection with our world exists.

"Tell me about your life this past week," I said to her. "How are things at home?"

"Oh, you wouldn't believe the things that have happened," she began. "What a bizarre week! First, while my boyfriend and I were watching TV on the couch, we heard a loud crash in the bathroom. When we went to see what had happened, you'll never guess what we saw."

"I couldn't begin to guess or even imagine," I said, "but now you've gotten me *really* interested . . . what happened?"

"Well, the hot-water pipe under the sink had exploded and blown the door of the vanity off its hinges and into the wall in front of the sink," she answered.

"Wow!" I exclaimed. "I've never heard of anything like that in my life."

"That's not all," she continued. "There's more! When we went to the garage to get the car, there was hot water all over the floor— the water heater had blown up and water was everywhere. Then, when we backed the car out of the garage into the driveway, the radiator hose on the car exploded, and there was hot antifreeze all over the driveway!"

I listened to what this woman was saying and immediately recognized the pattern. "What was going on at home that day?" I asked. "How would you describe your relationship?"

"That's easy," she blurted out. "It had been like a *pressure cooker* in that house." Suddenly, she became quiet and just looked at me. "You don't think that the tension in our relationship has anything to do with what happened, do you?"

"In my world," I replied, "it has *everything* to do with what happened. We're tuned to our world, and the world shows us physically the energy of what we experience emotionally.

Sometimes it's subtle, but in your case, it was literal—your house literally mirrored the strain that you just described between you and your boyfriend. And it did so through the very essence that has been used for thousands of years to represent emotion: the medium of water. What a powerful, beautiful, and clear message you've received from the field! Now, what will you do with it?"

> **Key 17:** The Divine Matrix serves as the mirror in our world of the relationships that we create in our beliefs.

Whether or not we recognize our resonant connection with the reality around us, it exists through the Divine Matrix. If we have the wisdom to understand the messages that come to us through our surroundings, our relationship with the world can be a powerful teacher. Sometimes it even saves our lives!

WHEN THE MESSAGE IS A WARNING

In my mother's life, next to her two sons, her very best friend has been a 12-pound bundle of energy wrapped up in the body of a border terrier named Corey Sue ("Corey," for short). While I travel frequently for tours and seminars, I do my best to call my mom at least once a week to check in and see how things are going in her life and let her know what's happening in mine.

Just before my 2000 book tour for *The Isaiah Effect*, I called home on a Sunday afternoon, and Mom shared her concerns about Corey. She hadn't been acting like herself or eating well, so my mother had taken her to a veterinarian to see if there was a problem. During the course of the examination, a series of x-rays were made, and they showed something that no one was expecting. For some unexplained reason, Corey's films showed patches of small white spots throughout her lungs that shouldn't have been there. "I've never seen anything like this in a dog before," the mystified vet had said. The decision was made to run further tests to see what the spots might be indicating about Corey.

While Mom was obviously worried about her dog, as I listened to her story, I became concerned for another reason. I shared the principle of resonance with her and how we're tuned to our world, our automobiles, our homes, and even our pets. I offered a number of case histories where animals have been documented to take on their owners' medical conditions weeks or even months before the same problems were found in the bodies of the people who cared for them. My sense was that something similar was happening with Corey and my mom.

After some convincing that life is full of such messages, Mom agreed to get a checkup for herself the following week. Although she was experiencing absolutely no discomfort, and from outward appearances she had no reason to have an examination, she agreed to schedule a physical that included a chest x-ray.

Well, you can probably tell where this story is headed and the reason why I'm sharing it here. To Mom's surprise, the x-rays revealed a suspicious spot on her lung, one that hadn't been there during her annual physical less than a year before. After further investigation, my mother discovered that she had scar tissue on her right lung from an illness that had healed during her childhood, and the spot had become cancerous. Three weeks later, she underwent surgery and the lower third of her right lung was completely removed.

As I spoke with the doctor in the recovery room afterward, he reiterated how "lucky" Mom was that the mass had been detected early on, especially since there were no telltale symptoms to alert her to any problems. Prior to the surgery, she'd felt great and was going through life with Corey, her sons, and her beautiful gardens with absolutely no clue that anything might be wrong.

This is an example of how we can apply the mirrors in our lives. Because Mom and I had learned to read the messages that life was showing us in the moment and we trusted the language enough to apply it in a practical way, this story has a happy ending: Mom recovered from her surgery. As of this writing, she's doing great and has been cancer free for six years.

Interestingly enough, the spots in Corey's lungs that had originally alerted us to investigate Mom's condition completely disappeared after the surgery as well. She and Mom had another six years together in good health, with all of the joy that they found in each other and their daily routines.

(*Note:* Corey Sue left this world during the editing of this book due to complications of her advanced age. When she died, halfway to her 15th birthday, she was nearly 100 in "dog years" for her breed. She lived out the period after her spots and Mom's surgery in good health and with a spark that brought joy to everyone whose life she touched. As Mom said many times, "No one was a stranger to Corey Sue." She loved everyone she met and let them know it with a gentle wet kiss that will be missed by all who knew her.)

While it may not be possible to prove scientifically that Corey's condition had anything whatsoever to do with what happened to my mother, we can say that the synchronicity between the two experiences is significant. And because this isn't an isolated incident, we have to say that when we see such synchronicities, there is a correlation. While we may not fully understand the connection today, the truth is that we could study it for another 50 years and still not comprehend it completely. What we *can* do is apply what we know in our lives. When we do, the events of every day become a rich language that offers insights into our most intimate secrets.

Once again, in a world where life itself mirrors our deepest beliefs, there can be few things that are truly secret. Ultimately, it probably matters less how the unexpected curves in the road of life come our way, and more, whether or not we recognize the language that warns us of them.

OUR GREATEST FEARS

Because the Divine Matrix constantly reflects our beliefs, feelings, and emotions through the events of our lives, the everyday world provides insights about the deepest realms of our hidden selves. In our personal mirrors, we're shown our truest convictions, loves, and fears. The world is a powerful (and often literal) mirror, one that isn't always easy to face. With complete honesty, life gives us a direct window into the ultimate reality of our beliefs, and sometimes our reflections come to us in ways that we would never expect.

I remember an incident that occurred in the Safeway grocery store of a Denver suburb one evening in 1989. I'd stopped on the way home from work as I often did to pick up a few things for dinner. As I wandered along the canned-food section, I glanced up from my grocery list just long enough to notice that I was alone in the aisle, except for a young mother with a small girl seated in her shopping cart. They were obviously in a hurry and looked as if they were about as happy to be grocery shopping at the end of their long day as I was.

As my attention returned to comparing the names on my list to those of the cans on the shelves, I was suddenly startled by the sound of a child's scream. This was not just any ol' shriek: The volume and intensity would have rivaled Ella Fitzgerald's "Is it live or is it Memorex?" commercials. The young girl was alone in the grocery cart, and she was terrified . . . absolutely terrified. Within a few seconds, the mother stepped into sight to calm her daughter down. Immediately, the child stopped screaming, and life returned to normal for everyone.

While we've all seen this before, something seemed different to me that night. For some reason, rather than simply ignoring such a common incident, I really took a look at what was happening. My eyes instinctively searched the aisle. All I saw was that the mother had momentarily stepped away from her cart, leaving her two- to three-year-old daughter by herself for a moment. That was all—the girl was simply alone.

Why was she so frightened? Her mother had just walked away for an instant out of sight around the corner of another aisle. Why would a young child, surrounded by a world of colorful cans and pretty labels and with no one around to discourage any exploration, be so frightened by such a situation? Why wouldn't she simply say to herself something along the lines of: *Hey, here I am alone with these beautiful red and white cans of Campbell's soup. I think I'll just explore each row, one can at a time, and have a great time doing it!* Why would the prospect of being alone, even if only for a moment, touch something so deep in her at that early age that her instinct would be to scream at the top of her lungs?

On another evening, I'd scheduled a counseling session with a woman in her mid-30s I'd worked with many times before. Our appointment began as usual: As the young woman relaxed into the wicker chair in front of me, I asked her to describe what had happened during the course of the week since we'd last talked. She began telling me about her relationship with her husband of nearly 18 years. For much of the marriage they'd fought, sometimes violently. She'd been on the receiving end of what seemed like daily criticism of everything from the way she dressed to how she ran the house and cooked the meals. Even in bed she said that she felt as though she was never good enough.

While the treatment she described was nothing new in their relationship, during the past week the situation had escalated. Her husband had become angry when she confronted him with questions about his "overtime" and late nights at the office. She was miserable with the man she'd loved and trusted for so long. Now her misery was being compounded with the very real threat of physical harm resulting from her husband's out-of-control emotions.

After knocking her to the ground in the heat of their most recent fight, her husband had left the house to go live with a friend. He provided no phone number, address, or indication of when or if he'd come back—he was just gone. The man who'd made this woman's life so miserable for so long and had threatened her safety with powerful outbursts of emotion and abuse was gone at last.

As she described his departure, I waited for some sign of relief. In its place, however, something astonishing started to happen. The woman began to sob uncontrollably with the realization that he was out of her life. When I asked her to describe how she was feeling, what I heard wasn't the resolution or relief that I'd expected. Instead, she said that she was experiencing the pain of loneliness and longing. She began to describe feeling "crushed" and "absolutely devastated" in the absence of her husband. Now, with the opportunity to live free of criticism, insults, and abuse, she was distressed. Why?

The answer to "why" in the two situations I just described is the same. As different as each one is from the other, a common thread runs through both of these situations. There's a very good chance that the terror that the young girl experienced in the supermarket aisle and the devastation felt by the woman whose abusive spouse walked out had little to do with the people who left them in those moments. The girl's mother and the woman's husband both served as catalysts for a subtle yet powerful pattern that runs so deep within each of us that it's nearly unrecognizable . . . often it's completely forgotten.

That pattern is fear.

And fear has many masks in our culture. Although it plays a key role in the way we build everything from our friendships and careers to our romances and the health of our bodies, fear surfaces almost on a daily basis as a pattern in our lives that we don't recognize. But interestingly, this pattern may not even be ours.

When we find ourselves touched by an experience that brings powerful negative emotions to the surface of our lives, we can rest assured that no matter what we *think* has caused fear to arise, there's a good possibility that something different is being played out—something so deep and primal that it's easy to overlook . . . that is, until it crosses our paths in a way that can't be mistaken.

OUR UNIVERSAL FEARS

If you're reading this book, the chances are good that you've already examined the many relationships in your life. In your explorations, you've no doubt gained valuable insights into which people have triggered certain emotions and why. In fact, you probably know yourself so well that if I asked you questions about your life and your past, you could give me just the right answers to arrive at just the right conclusions for any therapeutic quiz that might be offered. And it's in those perfect and acceptable answers that you may miss the single deepest pattern that's permeated your life from the day you were born. It's for this very reason that I invite seminar participants to complete a preprinted form asking them to identify the greatest patterns of their childhood caretakers that they would consider "negative."

I ask for the negative patterns because I've rarely seen people trapped in the positive patterns of joy in their lives. Almost universally, the situations that cause people to feel stuck have roots in what are considered negative feelings. These are the emotions that we have about our own experiences and what they mean to us in our lives. And while we can't alter *what* has happened, we can understand *why* we feel as we do and change what our life history means to us.

After completing the exercise, I ask the audience members to randomly shout out the characteristics that they've noted as negative qualities in both their male and female caretakers. In many people, these are their birth father and mother, while for others, they're their foster parents. To some, they're older brothers, sisters, other relatives, or family friends. Regardless of who it is, the question relates to the people who cared for them in their formative years—that is, until about the age of puberty.

Any shyness in the room disappears as people begin to yell out the negative qualities from their charts as quickly as I can write them on a whiteboard. Immediately, something interesting begins to happen: As one person shares the word that describe his or her memory, someone else offers the same feeling and often even that exact word. A sampling of the terms from any program shows nearly identical adjectives, including:

Angry	Cold	Unavailable	Critical
Judgmental	Abusive	Jealous	Strict
Controlling	Invisible	Fearful	Dishonest

There's a lightness that begins to fill the room, and people start to laugh at what they're seeing. If we didn't know better, we'd think that we all came from the same family. The similarity of the words is more than coincidence. How can so many people from such diverse backgrounds have such similar experiences? The answer to this mystery is the pattern that runs deeply in the fabric of our collective consciousness, which may be described as our core, or *universal,* fears.

Universal patterns of fear may be so subtle in their expression yet so painful to recall that we skillfully create the masks that make them bearable. Similar to the way a difficult family memory is always there yet seldom discussed, we have unconsciously agreed to disguise the hurt of our collective past in ways that are socially acceptable. We're so successful in concealing our greatest fears that for all intents and purposes, the original reasons for our hurts are forgotten, and all that remains is their expression—that is, to act them out.

Just as the woman losing her husband or the young girl in the supermarket probably weren't aware of why they felt and reacted as they did, neither are we. Due to the ways we mask our fear, we never have to talk about the deepest hurts of our lives. Yet they remain with us, lingering and unresolved, until something happens and we can no longer simply look in another direction. When we allow ourselves to go a little deeper into these powerful, unmasked moments of life, what we discover is that as different as all our fears appear to be, they resolve into one of only three basic patterns (or a combination of them): the fear of separation and abandonment, the fear of low self-worth, and the fear of surrender and trust.

Let's explore each one.

OUR FIRST UNIVERSAL FEAR:
SEPARATION AND ABANDONMENT

Almost universally there is a feeling that runs through each of us that we're alone. Within each person and every family, there's an unspoken sense that we're somehow separated from whomever or whatever is responsible for our existence. We feel that somewhere in the mists of our ancient memory we were brought here and then abandoned without any explanation or reason.

Why would we expect to feel any differently? In the presence of the science that can place a human on the moon and translate our genetic code, we still don't really know who we are. And we certainly don't know for sure how we got here. We sense our spiritual nature from within, while we look to validate our feelings. From literature and cinema to music and culture, we make a distinction between our places here on Earth and a distant heaven that's somewhere else. In the West, we affirm our separation from our Creator through our translation of the great prayer from the Bible that describes this relationship: The Lord's Prayer.

For example, the common Western translation begins: "Our Father, who art in Heaven," acknowledging this separation. In this interpretation, we're "here" while God is somewhere else far away. The original Aramaic texts, however, offer a different view of our relationship with our Heavenly Father. A translation of the same phrase begins, "Radiant One: You shine within us, outside us—even darkness shines—when we remember,"[2] reinforcing the idea that the Creator isn't separate and distant. Rather, the creative force of our Father—whatever the meaning we give to it—is not only with us, it *is* us and permeates all that we know as our world.

The 2004 discovery of the God Code and the message that comes from translating the DNA of all life into the letters of ancient Hebrew and Arabic alphabets seems to support this translation. When we follow the clues left to us in the 1st-century mystical book, the *Sepher Yetzirah,* we find that every one of the elements that compose our DNA corresponds to a letter from these alphabets. When we make the substitutions, we discover that the first layer of DNA in our bodies does, in fact, seem to support the ancient admonition that a great intelligence resides everywhere, including within us. Human DNA literally reads: *"God/Eternal within the body."*[3]

When we have a fear in our lives, even if we aren't consciously aware of precisely what it is, it creates an emotional bias in our bodies—an experience often described as a "charge" or a "hot button." This shows up in our lives as the strong ideas we have as to something's "rightness" or "wrongness," or the way that a situation "should" play out. Our charges and hot buttons are the promise that we'll create the relationships that show us which fear is asking to be healed. In other words, these charges will show us our fears—the greater one is, the deeper the fear. And they're seldom wrong.

So, if you don't consciously remember your fear of separation and abandonment, for example, there's a good possibility that it will show up in your life in ways that you least expect and during the times that are the most inconvenient. In your romances, careers, and friendships, for instance, do you find that you're the "leaver" or the "leavee"?

Are you the one who's always the last to know that the relationship is over? Do perfectly "good" marriages, jobs, and friendships seem to crumble before your eyes without warning and for no apparent reason? And are you devastated when these relationships break and fail?

Or maybe you're on the other side of this. Do you always leave your relationships, careers, and friendships while they're still going strong just to avoid being hurt? Do you find yourself saying something such as: "This is the perfect _____ [fill in the blank]. I'd better quit now while things are good, before something happens and I get hurt." If this kind of scenario has played out in your life or is doing so now, there's a good possibility that it's your masterfully created and socially acceptable way of masking your deepest fears of abandonment and separation.

By repeating these patterns in relationship after relationship, you may reduce the pain of your fear to a manageable level. It might even get you through your entire life. The trade-off, however, is that the suffering turns into a diversion. It becomes your way of looking away from the universal fear that you were separated from the wholeness of your Creator, abandoned and eventually forgotten. How can you ever find the love, trust, and closeness that you long for if you're always leaving or being left behind just when you get close?

OUR SECOND UNIVERSAL FEAR: LOW SELF-WORTH

Almost universally there is a feeling that runs through each person in every culture and society of our world that we are somehow just not good enough. We feel that we don't deserve recognition for our contributions to our families, communities, and workplaces. We feel that we aren't worthy of being honored and respected as human beings. Sometimes we even surprise ourselves with the feeling that we aren't good enough to be alive.

While this sense of low self-worth may not always be conscious, it's there continuously and provides the underlying foundation for the way we approach life and our relationships with other people. As masters of emotional survival, we often find ourselves playing out the real-life scenarios that equate to the imaginary values we place on ourselves.

For example, every one of us has dreams, hopes, and aspirations of accomplishing greater things in our lives, and more often than not we rationalize all the reasons why we'll never have them. As we've seen in earlier chapters, emotion is a language unto itself, the very language that the Divine Matrix responds to. When we feel as though we can't achieve our biggest dreams, the Matrix simply gives back to us what we've given it to work with: delays, challenges, and obstacles.

Although we may wish for greater things, the doubt that comes from deep within us ultimately comes from our feelings of low worth. We wonder, *Am I good enough to have such joy in my life?* And why would we expect to feel any differently? In the Western

Judeo-Christian tradition, we've been told by those we trust and respect that we're somehow "lesser" beings. We aren't as good as the angels of the heavens or the saints that we learn from. This same tradition has convinced many people that just by being in this world, we need to be redeemed from life itself for reasons that we're told are beyond our understanding.

Through the 2,000-year-old story of Jesus, we're compared to the edited, condensed, and preferred memory of a man's life that we can never live up to. Sometimes the comparisons are serious admonitions, suggesting that we may be condemned to a very tough afterlife if we don't live a certain way. Sometimes they're a little lighter, simply reminding us of our inadequacy by asking sarcastic questions such as: "Who do you think you are—Jesus Christ?" or "How are you going to get there . . . walk on water?" How many times have you heard these or similar remarks, implying that even though you may try your best to live a good life, you'll never be as good or worthy as a master of the past? Although we seldom take such comments seriously, on a deep level they still remind us that we're somehow undeserving of life's greatest joys.

Even if you have high self-esteem, to some degree you may believe these suggestions. Ultimately, on some level, we all probably do. As a result, we express our beliefs through our expectations of our achievements, how much joy we allow ourselves, and the success of our relationships. Our fear of not being valuable enough to have love, acceptance, health, and longevity promises that every one of our relationships will reflect the fear of low worth. And it happens in ways that we would never expect in a million years.

For example, how many times have you settled for relationships that aren't what you really want but rationalized them by saying things such as: "This is good enough for now" or "This is a stepping-stone to something better"? Have you ever found yourself saying, "I'd love to share my life with a loving, compassionate, nurturing, and caring partner, but . . ." or "This isn't the job where I can really express my gifts and talents, but . . ." followed by all the reasons why your greatest dreams can't be realized in this moment?

If these or similar scenarios have played out in your life, there's a good chance that they are the skillfully created masks that you use to question your worth. Through your personal and business relationships, you remind yourself of your core beliefs about yourself, beliefs that ask for a greater healing.

OUR THIRD UNIVERSAL FEAR: SURRENDER AND TRUST

Have you ever experienced a relationship of any kind where your level of trust was so complete that you were able to surrender your individual self in exchange for knowing a greater one? To be clear here, I'm not suggesting that you give yourself and all of your personal power away in any situation. On the contrary, the experience that I'm asking about is one where you have such a strong sense of who you are that you allow yourself to let go of your beliefs about what or who you should be in exchange for a greater possibility of what you may become.

Almost universally there's a feeling within each of us that it's not safe to do so—it isn't safe to trust other people, the wisdom of our bodies, or the peace of our world. And why should we think any differently? We need look no further than the evening news to give ourselves plenty of reasons to justify our feelings. Every day we're shown examples of behavior that seem to justify, and even perpetuate, the sense that we live in a frightening and dangerous world. From the terror, murder, and assaults that we see in the world at large to the violations of trust and betrayals that we experience in our personal lives and the myriad health concerns we're cautioned to watch for each day, this planet we call "home" certainly can look like a really scary place.

Ultimately, our sense of safety in the world must come from the security that we feel inside ourselves. To experience this, we must trust—we need to ask ourselves if we have faith in the intelligence of the universe that's inherent in all situations and all life. If our answer to this question is no, then we must ask ourselves *Why?* Who or what experience taught us that our world isn't safe and it's not okay to trust?

Do you believe in the process of life, for example? When you find that the universe has thrown an unexpected curveball at you, a loved one, or a pet, do you immediately go to a place of blame so that you can feel protected? When your children walk out the door to go to school in the morning, do you worry that something might happen and they won't be safe, or do you know that they're secure until you feel the joy of welcoming them home when the bus drops them off at 3:30 in the afternoon?

Although all of the frightening things that we see happening around us are certainly part of *a* reality, the key to overriding our fears is that they don't necessarily need be part of *our* reality. While this may seem like a naive New Age philosophy, it's actually a very ancient belief that's now supported by leading-edge science. We know that the Divine Matrix exists, reflecting in our lives whatever we think, feel, emote, and believe in our hearts and minds. We're aware that a subtle shift in the way we see ourselves is all that's needed for that change to be mirrored in our health, careers, and relationships. And this is where the preposterous nature of this vicious cycle of fear becomes apparent.

> **Key 18:** The root of our "negative" experiences may be reduced to one of three universal fears (or a combination of them): abandonment, low self-worth, or lack of trust.

If we want something to change, we have to break the cycle and give the Matrix something different to reflect. Sounds simple, doesn't it? It may be deceptively simple, since changing the way we see ourselves is probably the most difficult practice that we'll ever be faced with in our lives. Because of our inner beliefs, we experience in our outer world the grand battle that's playing out within the hearts and minds of every person alive—the struggle that defines who we believe we are.

In the presence of all the reasons *not* to trust, we're asked to find a way out of the prison that our fear locks us into. Each day, the experiences of life ask us to show ourselves how much we can trust . . . not simply to blindly trust for no reason, but to really feel the safety and security that are ours in the world.

CHAPTER SEVEN

READING THE MIRRORS OF RELATIONSHIP:
MESSAGES FROM OURSELVES

*"Life is a mirror and will reflect
back to the thinker
what he thinks into it."*
— Ernest Holmes (1887–1960),
founder of Science of Mind

*"The kingdom is inside of you,
and it is outside of you. . . .
There is nothing hidden
which will not become manifest."*
— Jesus's words, recorded by
Didymos Judas Thomas,
from the Nag Hammadi library

In addition to being the container for our experiences, the Divine Matrix provides the quantum mirror that shows us in our world what we've created in our beliefs. Through our relationships with other people, we're presented with the clearest examples of what those beliefs really are. Sometimes our mirrors are obvious, and we say, "So! That's the way things work." And other times they surprise us by reflecting the subtle reality of a judgment that's very different from what we'd *thought* we believed.

Regardless of what the mirrors teach us, it's by spending time with others that they become the triggers for just the right emotions and feelings at precisely the right times in our lives to help us heal our greatest hurts and deepest wounds. Our relationships show us our joys and loves, as well as our fears. But because we seldom become "stuck" in joy, purely pleasurable relationships are generally not the triggers for the profound lessons of life.

Relationships are our opportunity to see ourselves in every way imaginable. From the greatest betrayals of our trust to our most desperate attempts to fill our emptiness, everyone—including our co-workers, classmates, and life mates—shows us something about ourselves. If we have the wisdom to recognize the messages that are being mirrored to us, we discover the beliefs that cause the suffering in our lives.

I've met people who tell me that they're taking a break from all relationships or will never be in another one because they find them too painful. The truth is that we're always in a relationship with someone or something. Even if we live on a mountaintop and never see another human, we must still interact with that mountain and ourselves. In those interactions, we'll be shown the true reflection of our core beliefs. The reason? Our mirrors in the world never stop—they're always working. There's no escape! And the mirrors never lie.

Key 19: Our true beliefs are mirrored in our most intimate relationships.

The Divine Matrix provides a neutral surface that simply reflects what's projected onto it. The question is whether or not we understand its language. Perhaps a better way to ask this is: Do we recognize the messages that we're sending to ourselves *as* the Divine Matrix?

In the 20th century, Science of Mind founder Ernest Holmes stated, "Life is a mirror and will reflect back to the thinker what he thinks into it."[1] Numerous ancient traditions recognized this connection and valued the reflections of relationships as the path to wholeness and union with the Divine. In the Coptic, Gnostic, and Essene texts that were discovered as part of the Nag Hammadi library in 1945, for example, we're shown a series of mirrors that will face everyone at some point in their lives. Although they may always be present, it seems that there's an order to the way we'll recognize them.

In these spiritual traditions, it was believed that as our painful feelings are healed, we master the patterns that allow the hurt to exist. In other words, to overcome the fear that may be in our lives today, we must first master the patterns that allow it to exist.

FIVE ANCIENT MIRRORS OF RELATIONSHIP

The First Mirror: Reflections of the Moment

The Second Mirror: Reflections of What We Judge in the Moment

The Third Mirror: Reflections of What We've Lost, Given Away, or Had Taken from Us

The Fourth Mirror: Reflections of Our Dark Night of the Soul

The Fifth Mirror: Reflections of Our Greatest Act of Compassion

Figure 12. Our relationship mirrors listed in the order that we usually learn them. In general, the most obvious mirrors are recognized first, allowing the power of the deeper, subtler ones to emerge and become clear.

In the following sections, we'll explore the five mirrors of relationship from the most obvious to the most subtle. The resolution of each in sequence is the coded equation that allows for our greatest healing in the least amount of time. Scientific research has shown that as we change the way we feel about what's happened to us in our past, we change the chemistry of our bodies in the present. Living in a universe where the way we feel about ourselves is mirrored through the world around us, it becomes more important than ever to recognize what our relationships are saying to us and learn to read the messages of the Divine Matrix.

THE FIRST MIRROR:
REFLECTIONS OF THE MOMENT

*"You read the face of the sky and of
the earth, but you have not recognized
the one who is before you, and you do
not know how to read this moment."*[2]
— The Gospel of Thomas

Animals are great mirrors for triggering the subtle emotions that we call our "issues." In the innocence of just being who they are, they can ignite powerful feelings of control and judgment about the way things should or shouldn't be. Cats offer a perfect example.

My first experience with cats began in the winter of 1980. I was working for a petroleum company as a computer geologist and living in a small apartment in Denver. As a member of the newly formed technical-services department, I spent most of my days, evenings, and weekends learning the ins and outs of new computers and applying what I learned to the traditional concepts of petroleum geology. I hadn't really considered owning any pets simply because I was never home enough to care for one.

One weekend a friend was visiting and brought me an unexpected gift: a beautiful orange and blond kitten about five weeks old. He was the runt of the litter and named Tigger after the tiger in the classic *Winnie-the-Pooh* children's books. Even though I wasn't allowed to have a pet in my apartment, I was immediately drawn to Tigger and found that the big presence he carried in his small body added so much to my life that I missed him when he wasn't there. Telling myself it could be only temporary, I decided to bend the rules a bit and keep him. And just like that, Tigger and I were a family.

Immediately, I trained my new friend to honor the "forbidden zones" in our home. He was taught to stay off of the couches, counters, and the top of the refrigerator. Above all, he couldn't be perched in the windowsills for the world to see while I was at work. Each day I'd come home and he would be sleeping in one of our approved places. Everything seemed to be working out great with our secret relationship.

One day I came home from work earlier than usual. As I opened the door to my apartment, Tigger was awakened from a deep cat sleep right on the kitchen counter next to the sink—a spot we had definitely identified as being off-limits. He was as surprised to see me come through the door as I was to find him on the counter. Immediately, he jumped down, returned to his place on the bed, and waited to see what I would do. Now I was curious: Was this just a one-time incident, or was it an indication of what really happened when I left the house each day? Did he know my patterns so well that he would be in the right place at the right time just as I arrived home each evening?

That day I tried an experiment. Walking out to my balcony overlooking a beautiful greenbelt below, I slipped behind the drapes to hide and wait, pretending that I'd left for work. Within minutes, Tigger jumped from the bed and went directly into the kitchen. Believing that I was gone, he returned to his perch on the counter next to the toaster and the juice machine. He was so comfortable in this place that he began to nod off and was soon fast asleep next to the sink, somewhere he'd never go if he knew that I was home.

It was only when I spoke with friends who also had cats that I learned something probably every other owner of a feline has already discovered: You don't train a cat! While there are certainly exceptions, generally cats do what cats do. They like high places and will gravitate to the highest ones—the same countertops, refrigerators, and windowsills that are forbidden zones. Although they may honor our rules while in our presence, when they're alone, cats rule their own worlds.

THE MIRRORS ARE EVERYWHERE

The reason I share this story is because of what Tigger's behavior "did" to me. In his simply being who he was, I found myself frustrated almost to the point of anger. He would look me directly in the eyes, and I knew that he was aware of precisely where his boundaries were. Still, he acted against his training and did what he chose to do, when he chose to do it.

Perhaps not coincidentally, during the time of my challenges with Tigger, I noticed parallels with frustrations in my job. In fact, it seemed as if the people I was supervising were doing to me exactly what Tigger was: They were disregarding my instructions for our projects. Following a particularly rough afternoon, one of my co-workers came up to me and asked why I simply didn't just let her do her job. I had given her an assignment, and she felt that I was micromanaging her performance every step of the way. Later that evening, I walked into my apartment, and Tigger was in the forbidden zone of the kitchen counter once again. And this time when he looked at me, he didn't even bother to move. I was furious!

As I sat on the couch to think about what I was being shown, I noticed the parallels between Tigger's "disrespect" for my rules and what felt like the same attitude from my co-workers. Through two simultaneous although seemingly unrelated experiences, both Tigger and my co-workers had shown me something important about myself. Each had mirrored a pattern so subtle that I hadn't been conscious of it until that very moment. It was to become the first in a series of mirrors that I would have to recognize within myself before I could heal even more powerful and subtle ones in my other relationships.

During the 1960s and '70s, it was common for self-help professionals to say that if we don't like what the world is showing us, we should look at ourselves. They taught that everything from the anger of our co-workers to the betrayals of our trust is a reflection of our deepest beliefs. The patterns we identify with most strongly are often the ones we can't even see in our lives. This scenario is precisely what was happening with regard to Tigger and the people at work.

I'm not suggesting that my co-workers were aware of how they were mirroring me or how this pattern was playing out in my life—I'm almost certain that they weren't. It's simply that through the dynamics between us, I saw something about myself that they brought out in me. At that time in my life, it was the mirror of control. Because the reflection happened in the moment rather than hours or even days later, I could see the connection between my behavior and their reactions. Immediate feedback was the key to my lesson.

THE MIRROR OF THE MOMENT

We can see how important it is to recognize the relationship between what we do and what happens in the world if we look at the anthropological studies of hidden tribes in Asia. When explorers discovered one of the "lost" tribes (they were only lost to us, of course, as *they* knew precisely who they were and where they were located), they were surprised to find that the members made no connection between sexual intercourse and pregnancy. The lag time of months between the act of sex and the moment of birth was so great that the link between the two events wasn't obvious to them. This is the value of our mirrors—their immediacy helps us understand the real, underlying connections between seemingly disparate events.

If we're seeing our beliefs play out through our mirrors, then they're happening now. Any reflection we see affords us a precious moment of opportunity. Once it's recognized, a negative pattern can be healed in a heartbeat! To recognize it is the first clue about why it exists. More often than not, we find that the negative patterns mirrored in our lives are rooted in one of the three universal fears we explored in the last chapter.

When we see our beliefs reflected in real time in our relationships with others, we experience the first of our mirrors, and it's just that: the mirror of the moment. Sometimes, however, the reflection of the moment may be showing us something even subtler than what we're doing in our lives—sometimes it will reveal to us what we *judge* in our lives. When it does, we're experiencing the second mirror of relationship.

THE SECOND MIRROR: REFLECTIONS OF WHAT WE JUDGE IN THE MOMENT

> *"Recognize what is in your sight,*
> *and that which is hidden from*
> *you will become plain to you."*[3]
> — The Gospel of Thomas

In the 1970s, one of my martial-arts instructors shared the secret of reading an opponent: "Each person in competition is a mirror to you. As your personal mirror, your opponent will show you who you are in the moment. By observing how he approaches you, you're seeing his reaction to how he perceives you." Throughout my life, I've remembered my instructor's words and thought about them often. Later on I began to apply what he had said about competition in the dojo to the way people behave in life. In 1992, I found myself embroiled in an experience where this mirror made no sense at all . . . it was then that I discovered the subtlety of the second mirror of relationship.

In the fall of that year, three new people came into my life within a very short period of time. Through them, I would experience three of the most powerful—as well as painful—relationships that I've known as an adult. Although I didn't recognize it at the time, each person would become a master teacher for me in a way that I never imagined he or she would or could. Together, they taught me the single lesson that assured me that my life would never be the same again. Even though each relationship served as a mirror for me at precisely the right time, I initially didn't recognize what they were teaching me.

The first relationship was with a woman who had come into my life with such similar goals and interests to mine that we chose to live and work together. The second one was a new professional partnership that was to provide much-needed support for setting up and organizing seminars throughout the country. The third relationship was a combination of a friendship and business arrangement, which involved a man caretaking my property when I traveled for work in exchange for a place to live in one of my unused buildings that was under renovation.

The fact that these relationships came to me at the same time should have been my clue that something was up—something big. Almost immediately, all three began to test my patience, assertiveness, and resolve. I felt like these people were making me crazy! With each one, there were arguments and disagreements. Because I was traveling so much, my tendency was to discount the tensions and avoid looking for a resolution. I found myself taking a "wait-and-see" attitude until I returned from my next trip. When I did, things were always just the way I'd left them and sometimes even worse.

At that time, I had a routine that I followed when I came into the airport after each seminar. I would collect my gear from the baggage area, withdraw enough cash from the ATM for gas and a meal, and begin my four- to five-hour drive home. On one particular trip, however, something happened that brought everything in these relationships to a focus. After collecting my bags, I went to the ATM to make my withdrawal. To my horror, the machine quietly printed a receipt that told me my account didn't even have enough money for a $20 bill for gas!

This was especially horrifying, because I'd recently scheduled contractors to begin renovations on the 100-year-old adobe buildings on my property, and they'd just been paid with checks written on that very account. In addition to mortgage, office, travel, and family expenses, the machine was telling me that there was nothing—absolutely nothing—to cover any of my other obligations. I knew that it had to be a mistake. I also knew that at 5:30 P.M. on a Sunday afternoon in New Mexico nothing could be done—everything was closed until Monday. After convincing the lot attendant that I would repay the long-term-parking bill by mail, I began my extended drive home and thought about what had happened.

When I called my bank the next morning, I got even more of a surprise. To my disbelief, the zero balance was no mistake; there was truly nothing there. In fact, there was less than nothing—an unauthorized withdrawal by the woman I had entrusted with my business had completely emptied my account. Because of the penalties that had been applied to each one of the overdrawn checks, I also suddenly found myself with a negative balance caused by hundreds of dollars in overdraft charges.

I felt shock and disbelief. Quickly my emotions turned to anger, and then the anger became rage. My mind raced with the thoughts of all the people whom I'd written checks to and how I couldn't honor those obligations. The violation of my trust and complete disregard for me and my commitments was more painful than I expected.

To make matters worse, later that day my business partnership reached a boiling point. As I opened my mail and looked over an accounting for seminars that I had already completed, I found discrepancies in the expenses, and soon I was on the phone fighting for my share of our proceeds, line item by line item.

During the same week, I discovered that the tenant living on my property was pursuing interests that were not only in direct opposition to the agreements that we had made, but they were also frowned upon by the state of New Mexico. Clearly, I could no longer ignore what was happening in any of my relationships.

THERE'S MORE THAN ONE MIRROR

The next morning, I walked down the dirt road leading away from my property to a large mountain that looms over the valley behind my home. In silent prayer, I stepped carefully over the deep mud ruts and broken gravel, asking for the wisdom to recognize the pattern that I was being shown so blatantly even though I couldn't see it. What was the common thread that wove these relationships together? Remembering what my martial-arts instructor had said, I asked myself, *What is the common reflection that these three people are showing me through their actions?*

Immediately, words began to race through my mind, some so quickly that they disappeared, while others stood out clearly. Within seconds, four words emerged above all others: *honesty, integrity, truth,* and *trust.* I asked myself more questions: *If these people are mirroring what I am in the moment, are they showing me that I'm dishonest? Have I somehow violated integrity, trust, and truth in my work?*

As I asked the questions in my mind, a feeling welled up from deep within my body. Inside of me, a voice—*my voice*—was screaming, *No! Of course I'm honest! Of course I have integrity! Of course I'm truthful and trustworthy! These things are the very basis of the work that I share with other people.*

In the very next moment, another feeling came over me— fleeting at first, then clearer and stronger, until it was solidly present for me to see and know. In that moment, the mirror suddenly became crystal clear: The three people I had so skillfully drawn into my life weren't showing me what *I was in the moment;* instead, each one of them was showing another, more subtle reflection that no one had told me about. Through our clashes of belief and lifestyle, rather than showing to me what I am, *they were showing me the things that I judge!* These individuals were showing me the qualities that triggered a big charge in me—the very qualities that I felt they'd violated.

At that time in my life, I did have an enormous judgment on the way people held themselves accountable to the attributes of honesty and integrity. In all probability, my charge had been building since childhood. In a moment, my past experiences suddenly became clear. Immediately, I remembered all the times that these same qualities had been violated in my life: past romances in which my partners weren't truthful about other people in our lives, adult promises that were made and never honored, well-intentioned friends and corporate mentors who'd made promises that they could never keep in a million years . . . my list went on and on.

My judgments regarding these issues had been building for years on such a minute level that I hadn't even recognized them. Now they were at the core of something I couldn't ignore! The magnitude of having an empty bank account was the assurance that I would have to understand the message of these relationships before I could move on in life. That was the day I learned the subtle yet profound mystery of the second mirror of relationship: the mirror of the things that I judge in life.

DO YOU RECOGNIZE YOUR MIRRORS?

I invite you to examine your relationships with the people who are closest to you. Next, acknowledge the traits and characteristics that irritate you to no end and just seem to make you crazy. Once you do so, ask yourself the following question: *Are these people showing me myself in this moment?*

They may very well be. If so, you'll know it as your "gut" feeling immediately. However, if the answer is no, they may be revealing something even deeper and more powerful than the mirror of who you are—they might be showing you the reflection of the things that you judge in life. To simply recognize and acknowledge that the mirror exists is where the healing of your judgments begins.

HEALING WITH THE CASCADE EFFECT

The day after I recognized the mirror of my judgments, I visited a friend who lives and works on the nearby Taos Pueblo. One of the oldest indigenous communities in North America, this site has been continuously inhabited for at least 1,500 years. Robert (not his real name) had a shop within the Pueblo itself and was a tremendously skilled artist and craftsman. Displayed throughout his store were the sculptures, dream catchers, music, and jewelry that had been part of his tradition for centuries before there was ever an "America."

As I walked in, he was working on a sculpture nearly seven feet tall that was standing in the aisle beside him. After saying our hellos, I asked about his family and how business had been, and we enjoyed a few minutes of catch-up talk. He returned my questions, asking me what was happening in my life. I shared the events of the past week, the three people, and the missing money. After listening to my account, he thought for a few moments and then told me a story.

"My great-grandfather," he began, "hunted buffalo on the plains of northern New Mexico." I knew that he must have been talking about a long time ago, because as far as I knew, no buffalo had roamed that part of the state for years. "Before his death, he gave me his most valuable possession: the head of the first buffalo that he ever hunted as a young boy." Robert went on to tell me how this buffalo head had become a treasure of his as well. After his great-grandfather died, it was one of the few tangible relics that connected him with the heritage of his past.

One day a gallery owner had come to visit Robert from the nearby town. Seeing how beautiful the head was, she asked if she could use it as part of a display in her gallery, and he had agreed. After a few weeks had passed, Robert hadn't heard from his friend and went into town to see how she was doing. To his surprise, when he arrived at the gallery, nothing was there. The doors were locked, the windows were covered, and the shop was out of business. The gallery owner and his buffalo head were both gone. Robert looked up from his sculpting long enough for me to see that he had been hurt in the experience.

"What did you do?" I asked. I expected to hear how he'd tracked down the gallery owner and retrieved his prized possession.

As his eyes met mine, the wisdom of his answer was not lost in its simplicity: "I did nothing, because she lives with what she has done." I left the Taos Pueblo that day thinking about the story and what it meant for my life.

Later that week, I began to explore the legal options for recovering at least some of the money that had disappeared from my account. I quickly learned that although I did have a good case, I was looking at a lengthy, drawn-out, and expensive process. Due to the nature of what had happened, I would be required to turn the case over to the authorities as a criminal, rather than a civil, matter. From that point on, it would be entirely out of my hands, and if convicted, the woman responsible could face prison time. All of this added up to a prolonged emotional relationship with someone whom I no longer felt any connection with.

As I thought about the options, I reflected once again on my conversation with my friend at the Pueblo and the lessons that had been learned. It didn't take long for me to reach a conclusion that immediately felt right: I chose to do nothing. Almost immediately, something unexpected began to happen—each of the three people mirroring my judgments began to fall away from my life. I was no longer angry with them, and I no longer resented them. I began to feel an odd sense of "nothingness" with regard to each of these three people. There was no intentional effort on my part to drive them away. After I redefined what had happened between us for what the experiences were and not what my judgments had made them out to be, there was simply nothing left to keep those people in my life. Each one simply began to fade from my day-to-day activities. Suddenly, there were fewer phone calls and letters from them, along with fewer thoughts about them throughout the course of the day. My judgments had been the magnet that had held those relationships in place.

While this new development was interesting, within a few days, something even more intriguing and even a little curious began to occur. I realized that there were other people who had been in my life for a long time who also began to fade away. Once again, there was no conscious effort on my part to end these relationships; they just didn't seem to make sense anymore. On the rare occasion that I did have a conversation with one of these individuals, it felt strained and artificial. Where there had been common ground before, now there was uneasiness.

Almost as soon as I noticed the shift in these relationships, I became aware of what for me was a new phenomenon. Each of the relationships that were falling from my life had been based in the same pattern that had originally brought the three people into my life . . . that pattern was judgment. In addition to being the magnet that drew the relationships to me, my judgment had also been the glue that had held them together. In its absence, the glue dissolved. I noticed what appeared to be a cascading effect: Once the pattern was recognized in one place—in one relationship—its echo faded on many other levels of my life.

The mirrors of judgment are subtle, elusive, and possibly won't make sense to everyone who becomes aware of them. When my friends and family heard of my decision to "do nothing," they felt that I was in denial about what had happened. "She took your money!" they said. "She violated your trust! She left you with nothing!" On one level, their observations were true enough—all of those things had happened. My sense was that if I had followed the typical pattern of retribution and getting even, I would have found myself in the vicious cycle of thinking that feeds just such an experience. On another level, however, in simply being who they were, each of the three people showed me something about myself that would become key in the business decisions that I would make in the future. That something was a powerful lesson in the discernment of trust.

Prior to that time, I'd wanted to believe that trust is binary. That is, we either trust someone or we don't—and if we do, we can trust them fully. While I didn't like to think of the world in another way, I had learned from these three relationships that there are levels of trust that we're left to discern in one another. Often we trust others to a greater degree and with more responsibility than they can even trust themselves. And this is just what I'd experienced.

The recognition of judgment reflected in a relationship is a powerful discovery that has reverberations that will touch every aspect of life. To the people who helped me with my lessons, I give thanks. And to those who showed me my humanness, I offer my deepest respect and gratitude for impeccably holding up the mirror before me. What a beautiful validation of the mystery of the second mirror of relationship!

(*Note:* In the previous story, I've alluded to reconciling the charge of judgment without fully describing precisely how that reconciliation may be accomplished. It is addressed fully in my 2006 Hay House release, *Secrets of the Lost Mode of Prayer,* as "The Third Secret: Blessing Is the Release." To summarize this powerful key to transforming our judgments, blessing is the ancient secret that releases us from life's suffering long enough to replace it with another feeling. When we bless the people or things that have hurt us, we're temporarily suspending the cycle of pain. Whether this suspension lasts for a nanosecond or an entire day makes no difference. Whatever the period of time, during the blessing a doorway opens for us to begin our healing and move on with life. The key is that for some interval, we're released from our hurt long enough to let something else into our hearts and minds: the power of "beauty.")

THE THIRD MIRROR: REFLECTIONS OF WHAT WE'VE LOST, GIVEN AWAY, OR HAD TAKEN FROM US

"The kingdom of the [father] is like a certain woman who was carrying a [jar] full of meal. While she was walking [on the] road, still some distance from home, the handle of the jar broke, and the meal emptied out behind her [on] the road. She did not realize it; she had noticed no accident. When she reached her house, she set the jar down and found it empty."[4]
— The Gospel of Thomas

Your love, compassion, and caring are like the meal in the jar of the preceding parable. Throughout your life, they are the parts of you that comfort, nurture, and support others (as well as *you*) in the tough times. When we lose the people, places, and things that we hold dear, it's our loving and compassionate nature that allows us to survive and get through those experiences.

Because we share them willingly, love, compassion, and caring are also the parts of us that are most vulnerable to being lost, innocently given away, or taken from us by those who have power over us. Each time we trust enough to love or nurture someone else and that faith is violated, we lose a little of ourselves to the experience. Our reluctance to expose ourselves again to such vulnerability is our protection—the way we survive our deepest hurts and greatest betrayals. And each time we shut off the access to our truest nature of compassion and nurturing, we're like the meal slowly leaving the jar that the woman is carrying.

When we do reach a point in life when we really want to open up and share ourselves with another person, we reach inside for our love, only to find that it's gone and has left a reservoir of emptiness in its place. We discover that we've lost ourselves little by little to the very experiences that we trusted enough to allow them into our lives.

The good news here is that those parts of ourselves that *seem* to be absent are never really gone. It isn't as though they're obliterated forever . . . they're part of our truest essence, a part of our soul. And just as the soul can never be destroyed, the core of our true nature can never be lost. It's simply masked and hidden for safekeeping. To recognize how we do the masking is to embark upon a fast path of healing. Calling back to us the parts of ourselves that we've lost may be the greatest expression of our personal mastery.

Early in my career in the defense industry, I worked as part of a team developing software for weapon systems. My colleagues and I shared a small work space in typical Air Force–regulation desks, chairs, and cubicles; and we spent long hours together in close proximity. As you can imagine, there was little privacy. As the phone conversations bounced from the stark Sheetrock walls and drifted over the tops of the cubicles, we got to know one another very well—so well, in fact, that we quickly became virtual advisors to one another for everything from career choices and dating options to family matters and personal lives.

Several times each week, we would go for lunch together, occasionally cashing paychecks and running quick noontime errands. It was during one of those lunch-hour adventures that I had the opportunity to see firsthand the mirror of an experience that created a personal "hell" in the life of one of my colleagues, a man who had also become a friend.

On any given day, my friend would "fall in love" with the women he met throughout the course of his business. It might be the server who had taken our order or the cashier at the checkout line of the grocery store. Honestly, it was almost anyone who crossed his path during the day (anyone female, that is). It happened everywhere, and the pattern was always the same: He would simply look into the woman's eyes and "feel this feeling" that he couldn't explain. Without understanding what it was all about, he placed his experience into the only explanation that he could find for what was happening. He felt that he was in love! And he fell in love many times each day.

The reason why this was such a problem was that he was married. He had a beautiful wife who loved him very much and a beautiful new son, and he loved both of them tremendously. The last thing he would ever want to do was hurt them in any way or destroy what they'd created together. At the same time, his feelings for other women were nearly overwhelming and something that he simply didn't understand.

On this occasion, we had just returned to the office following a quick lunch and gas-station/bank run. It was in the bank that he got into trouble. There was a beautiful teller working at the window where we deposited our checks. (This was in the old days before electronic deposits.) By the time we got back to the office, all he could do was think about her. He couldn't work or focus, and he was unable to get her off his mind. "What if she's thinking about me right now?" he asked. "What if she's 'the one'?" Finally, he picked up the phone, called the bank, found the teller, and asked if they could meet for coffee after work. She agreed. But while they were at the coffee shop, he looked into the eyes of the woman serving the drinks and fell in love with *her!*

I'm sharing this story because for reasons that he didn't understand, this man was compelled to initiate contact with women he honestly believed he had feelings for. In doing so, he was risking everything that he held dear, including his wife, son, and career. What was happening to him?

Have you ever had a similar experience (although hopefully to a lesser degree)? Have you ever found yourself in a perfectly happy, committed relationship, and suddenly "it" happens? Or maybe you're not in a relationship or even looking for one, when—without warning—there you are walking down a busy street or in a mall, grocery store, or airport, and you have "the experience." Someone you've never seen before passes you, in that instant your eyes meet, and—*zing*—there's that feeling. Perhaps it's just a sense of familiarity or possibility, or it could be a nearly overwhelming impulse to stand close to this person, to get to know him or her, or even to initiate a conversation. I've asked about this many times in workshop situations. Interestingly, I've found that if we're really honest with ourselves, this kind of connection isn't so unusual.

When it happens, the encounter commonly goes something like this: Even though two people's eyes have met and they've obviously felt the "feeling," one of them will discount the moment. For a brief fraction of a second, however, something undeniable happens . . . there's an altered state and a sense of unreality. In that fleeting instant beyond the casual glance, their eyes communicate a message. Each person will be saying something to the other in that moment that probably neither is even aware of.

Then, almost as if on cue, their rational minds will create a distraction—anything to break the uneasiness of the contact. It may be the sound of a car or another person passing by. It can be as simple as a leaf blowing across the street, or a sneeze. It could even be sidestepping gum on the sidewalk! The point is that using anything for an excuse, one of the people will shift his or her attention, and the moment will be gone, just like that!

When we have such an experience, what has just happened?

FINDING WHAT WE'VE LOST IN OTHER PEOPLE

When we find ourselves in these situations, we're faced with a powerful opportunity to know ourselves in a very special way— that is, if we recognize what the moment is all about. If we don't, then, as my engineer friend discovered, this kind of connection can become confusing and even frightening! The secret of such encounters is the essence of the mystery of the third mirror.

To survive in our lives, we've all compromised huge parts of who we are. Each time we do so, we lose something inside in ways that are socially acceptable, yet nonetheless painful. Taking on adult roles and missing out on childhood following a family breakup; the loss of racial identity as cultures are forced together; and the survival of an early trauma through repressing emotions of hurt, anger, and rage are all examples of losing pieces of ourselves.

Why would we do such a thing? Why would we betray our beliefs, love, trust, and compassion, knowing that they're the very essence of who we are? The answer is simple: It's survival. As a child, we may have discovered that it's easier to remain silent, rather than voicing an opinion at the risk of being ridiculed and invalidated by parents, brothers, sisters, and peers. As the object of abuse in a family, it's much safer to "give in" and forget, instead of resisting those who have power over us. As a society, we accept the killing of others during war, for example, and justify it as a special circumstance. We've all been conditioned to give ourselves away in the face of conflict, disease, and overwhelming emotion in ways that we're only now beginning to understand. In each instance, we have the opportunity to see a powerful possibility, rather than the judgment of what's right and wrong.

For every piece of ourselves that we've given away to be where we are in life today, there's the emptiness that's left behind, waiting to be filled. We're constantly searching for whatever it is that fills our particular void. When we find someone who has the very things that we've given away, it feels good to be near him or her. The person's complementary essence fills our inner void and makes us feel whole again. This is the key to understanding what happened to my engineer friend and in the other examples previously discussed.

When we find our "missing" pieces in others, we'll be powerfully and irresistibly drawn to them. We may even believe that we "need" them in our lives, until we remember that what we're so attracted to in them is something that we still have within us . . . it's simply sleeping. In the awareness that we still possess those characteristics and traits, we may unmask them and reincorporate them back into our lives. And when we do, we suddenly find that we're no longer powerfully, magnetically, and inexplicably drawn to the person who originally mirrored those traits for us.

Recognizing our feelings toward others for what they are and not for what our conditioning has made them out to be is the key to the third mirror of relationship. That unexplainable feeling that we have when we're with someone else—that magnetism and fire that makes us feel so alive—is really *us!* It's the essence of those parts of us that we've lost and our recognition that we want them back in our lives. So, with this in mind, let's go back to the story of my engineer friend.

Certainly, there's a good possibility that without knowing it consciously, my friend had seen in those women pieces of himself that he had lost, given away, or had taken from him throughout his life. There's a good chance that he ran across them in men as well, but couldn't allow himself to have the same feelings because of his conditioning. In his experience, the things that he lost were so prevalent that he found some trace of them in nearly everyone he met.

Not understanding what his feelings were all about, however, he was compelled to follow them in the only way he knew. He honestly believed that each encounter was an opportunity for happiness, because he felt so good while he was with the women. He still loved his wife and son very much—when I asked him once if he would ever leave them, he looked shocked. He had no desire to end his marriage, yet he followed the force of what he felt into compromising situations until the loss of his family became a very real danger.

HOW TO DISCOVER WHAT YOUR FEELINGS OF ATTRACTION ARE TELLING YOU

Each of us has masterfully given away the portions of ourselves that we felt were necessary in the moment for our physical or emotional survival. When we do, it's easy to see ourselves as "less than" and get trapped within our beliefs about what remains. For some people, the trade-off occurs before we ever know it, and we don't realize what's happened; for others, it's a conscious choice.

One afternoon while I was working in the same defense corporation with my engineer friend, an unexpected invitation landed on my desk. It was for an informal presentation that was to be made to White House and military officials for the newly funded weapon system named Strategic Defense Initiative (SDI), popularly referred to as "Star Wars." During the reception that followed the event, I had the opportunity to listen in on a conversation between one of the high-ranking military officials and a CEO from our company.

The question that the CEO asked related to the personal cost the other man had incurred to be in his position of power. "What sacrifices did you have to make to get where you are today?" he asked. The official described how he'd risen through the ranks of the military and the Pentagon and into a position of authority with a large multinational corporation. I listened intently as the man answered with unusual candor and honesty.

"To get where I am today," he began, "I had to give myself away to the system. Each time I advanced in rank, I lost another piece of myself in life. One day I realized that I was on top and looked back at my life. What I discovered was that I'd given away so much of myself that there was nothing left. The corporations and military owned me. I'd let go of the things that I loved the most: my wife, children, friends, and health. I traded those things for power, wealth, and control."

I was amazed by his honesty. Even though this man had admittedly lost himself in the process, he was aware of what he'd done. He was saddened, but to him it was a price worth paying for his position of power. Although probably not for the same reasons, we each may do something similar over the course of our lives. For many of us, however, the goal is less about power and more about survival.

When you do encounter someone in your life who ignites a feeling of familiarity, I invite you to immerse yourself in the moment. Something rare and precious is happening for both of you: You've just found someone who's kept the pieces of you that you're searching for. Often this is a two-way experience, with the other person being drawn to you for the same reason! Using your power of discernment, if you feel that it's appropriate, initiate a conversation. Begin talking about anything—anything at all—to maintain eye contact. While you're speaking, mentally ask yourself this simple question: *What do I see in this person that I've lost in myself, given away, or had taken from me?*

Almost immediately, a response will come to you in your mind. It may be something as simple as a feeling of realization or as clear as a voice within that you recognize and that's been with you since childhood. Answers are often single words or short phrases, and your body knows what's meaningful for you. Maybe you simply perceive a beauty in this person that you feel is missing within you for the moment. Possibly it will be the individual's innocence in life, the grace with which he or she moves down the grocery aisle, his or her confidence while performing the task at hand, or simply the radiance of his or her vitality.

Your encounter need last only seconds, perhaps a few minutes at most. Those brief instants are your opportunity to feel the joy and exhilaration of the moment. This is you finding part of yourself in another person, something that you already have, as well as the feeling of what it's like to have that something awakened.

For those of us who dare to acknowledge the sense of familiarity in such momentary encounters, the mirror of loss is probably something that faces us every day. We find a completeness in ourselves as others mirror to us our truest nature. Collectively, we're looking for our wholeness, and we individually create the situations that lead us to find it. From members of clergy to teachers, older people to youthful individuals, parents to children, all are catalysts of feeling.

In those feelings, we find the things that we long for in ourselves, the things that are still with us yet are hidden in our masks of who we believe we are. It's natural and human. Understanding what our feelings about others are really saying about us may become our most powerful tool in discovering our greatest power.

THE FOURTH MIRROR:
REFLECTIONS OF OUR DARK NIGHT OF THE SOUL

*"That which you have will save you
if you bring it forth from yourselves."*[5]
— The Gospel of Thomas

During the high-tech boom of the early 1990s, Gerald (not his real name) was an engineer in Silicon Valley, California. He had two beautiful young daughters and was married to an equally beautiful wife. They'd been together for nearly 15 years. When I met him, his company had recently given him an award for his fifth year with them as a senior troubleshooter for a specialized kind of software. His position had made him a valuable asset to the company, and the need for his expertise extended well beyond the typical 8-to-5 workday.

To meet the demand for his skills, Gerald began to work late evenings and weekends and travel to trade shows and expos out of town with his software. Before long, he found himself spending more time with his co-workers than he did with his family. I could see the hurt in his eyes as he described how they'd grown apart. By the time Gerald arrived home in the evenings, his wife and children were sleeping, and he was at his office in the morning before they even started their day. Soon he began to feel like a stranger in his own home. He knew more about the families of people in his office than he did his own.

That's when Gerald's life took a dramatic turn. He happened to come to see me for a counseling session while I was writing a book entitled *Walking Between the Worlds: The Science of Compassion,* describing how the "mirrors" of relationships play out in our lives. More than 2,200 years ago, the authors of the Dead Sea Scrolls identified seven specific patterns that we may expect to see in our interactions with other people. As Gerald's story unfolded, it was clear that he was describing one of them, which is life's reflection of our greatest fear, commonly known as the "Dark Night of the Soul."

Among the engineers in his office was a brilliant young programmer who was about his age. He'd found himself teamed up with this woman for assignments that sometimes lasted for days at a time and took them to cities throughout the country. Before long, he felt as though he knew her better than he did his own wife. At this point in the story, I suspected that I knew where it would end. What I didn't know was what happened next and why Gerald was so upset.

Before long, he believed that he was in love with his co-worker and made the choice to leave his wife and daughters to begin a new life with her. This decision made perfect sense at the time, as they had so much in common. Within a few short weeks, however, his new partner was transferred to a project in L.A. By calling in a few favors, Gerald was able to finagle a transfer to the same office.

Immediately, things began to go wrong, and Gerald found that he'd lost more than he'd bargained for. Friends that he and his wife had known for years suddenly became distant and unavailable. His co-workers thought he was "off the wall" for leaving the position and projects that he'd worked so hard for. Even his parents were angry that he'd broken up the family. Although he was hurt, Gerald rationalized that this was simply the price of change. He was off to a great new life. What more could he ask for?

This is where the mirror of balance and the Dark Night of the Soul come in. Just as everything appeared to be falling into place, Gerald discovered that everything was actually falling apart! Within weeks, his new love announced that their relationship wasn't what she'd expected. She ended it suddenly and asked him to leave. Just like that, he was on his own, alone and devastated. "After all that I've done for *her*, how could she?" he moaned. He'd left his wife, children, friends, and job—in short, he'd surrendered everything that he loved.

Soon he began to perform poorly at his job. Following several warnings and a less-than-stellar performance review, his department eventually laid him off. As Gerald's story unfolded, it was clear what had really happened: His life had gone from the highest of highs, with all the prospects of a new relationship, new job, and greater income, to the lowest of lows, as all of those dreams disappeared. The night that Gerald came to see me, he was asking a single question: "What happened?" How could things that looked so good have turned out so bad?

OUR DARK NIGHT OF THE SOUL: RECOGNIZING THE TRIGGER

By the time I met him, Gerald had lost everything that he loved. The reason why is the key to this story. Rather than releasing the things he loved *because* he felt complete and was moving on, he made his choices only when he believed that there was something better to take their place. In other words, he played it safe. Because of his fear that he might not find anything better, he physically stayed with his marriage and family long after he'd left emotionally. There's a subtle yet significant difference between leaving our jobs, friends, and romances because we're complete and staying with them because of the fear that there's nothing else for us!

There can be a tendency in all kinds of relationships to cling to the status quo until something better comes along. This attachment may come from being unaware of what we're doing, or it may exist because we're afraid to rock the boat and face the uncertainty of not knowing what comes next. Although it may very well represent a pattern that we aren't conscious of, it's a pattern nonetheless. Whether it's a job, a romance, or our lifestyle, we can find ourselves in a holding pattern where we aren't really happy yet have never honestly communicated this to the people in our lives. So even while the world believes that our lives are business as usual, inside we may be screaming for change and feeling frustrated because we don't know how to share this need with those who are close to us.

This is a pattern that builds negativity. Our true feelings are disguised as tension, hostility, or sometimes just being absent from the relationship. Each day we go through the motions of our job or of sharing our life and home with another person, while we're emotionally distant and off in another world. Whether our problem is with a boss, a lover, or even ourselves, we rationalize, compromise, and wait. Then one day, just like that—*boom!*—it happens. Seemingly from out of nowhere, the very things that we've waited and longed for in our lives suddenly appear. When they do, we may lunge for them like there's no tomorrow.

In Gerald's case, when he moved to a new city with his new relationship, he left behind an unresolved void into which his world collapsed. Now, having lost all that he loved, Gerald sat across from me with huge tears rolling down his cheeks. "How can I get back my job and my family? Just tell me what to do!"

As I handed him the box of tissues that I kept on the nearby table for moments just like this one, I said something that caught Gerald completely off guard: "This time in your life isn't about getting back what you've lost, although that may be just what happens. What you've created for yourself goes much deeper than your job and your family. You've just awakened a force within you that may become your most powerful ally. When you've come through this experience, you'll have a new confidence that's unshakable. You've entered a time the ancients recognized and called the Dark Night of the Soul."

Gerald wiped his eyes and sat back in his chair. "What do you mean the 'Dark Night of the Soul'?" he asked. "How come I've never heard of it?"

"A Dark Night of the Soul is a time in your life when you'll be drawn into a situation that represents what, for you, are your worst fears," I answered. "A time like this generally comes when you least expect it, and usually without warning. The thing is," I continued, "you can only be drawn into this dynamic when your mastery of life signals that you're ready! Then, just when it looks like life is perfect, the balance that you've achieved is the signal that you're ready for change. The lure to create the change will be something that you long for in life, something that you simply can't resist. Otherwise, you'd never take the leap!"

"Do you mean a lure like a new relationship?" Gerald asked.

"Precisely like a new relationship," I replied. "A relationship is the kind of catalyst that promises we'll move forward in life." I went on to explain how even if we know that we're perfectly capable of surviving whatever life throws our way, it's not our nature to wake up one morning and say, "Hmm . . . today I think I'll give away all that I love and hold dear to enter my Dark Night of the Soul." We just don't seem to work that way! As is so often the case, the great tests of our Dark Night seem to come at a time when we least expect them.

The possibility that life brings us exactly what we need precisely when we need it makes perfect sense. Just as we can't fill a cup with water until we turn the tap to "on," having a full emotional toolbox is the trigger that signals the faucet of life to bring on change. Until we trigger the flow, nothing can happen. The flip side of this dynamic is that when we do find ourselves in a Dark Night of the Soul, it may be reassuring to know that the only way we could have gotten to such a place in life is that *we* were the ones who flipped the switch. Knowingly or not, we're always ready for whatever life may serve.

OUR GREATEST FEARS

The purpose of the Dark Night of the Soul is for us to experience and heal our own great fears. The really interesting thing about the Dark Night is that because everyone's fears are different, what looks like a frightening experience for one person may be no big deal to someone else. For example, Gerald admitted that his worst fear was being left by himself. I'd spoken with a woman earlier the same evening who told me that "being alone" was her greatest joy.

It's not uncommon for someone who fears being alone to become a master at relationships in which they'll experience their fear. Gerald, for example, described romances, friendships, and jobs in his past that never could have lasted in a million years! Yet when each one ended, he believed that the relationship had "failed." In reality, they were so successful that each allowed him to see his greatest fear of being alone come to pass. Because he'd never healed or even recognized the patterns in his life before, however, he found himself in situations where his fear became less and less subtle. Ultimately, life led him to the point where this emotion was so present that he had to address it before he could continue.

⸺⸺⸺⸺⸺⸺

While we may go through many Dark Nights of the Soul throughout our lifetimes, the first one is usually the toughest. It's also frequently the most powerful agent of change. Once we understand *why* we hurt so much, the experience begins to take on new meaning. As we recognize the signposts of a Dark Night, we can say, "Aha! I know that pattern! Yup, it's definitely a Dark Night of the Soul all right. Now, what is it that I'm being asked to master?"

I know people who are so empowered once they heal their Dark Night experiences that they almost dare the universe to bring on the next one! They do so simply because they know that if they've survived the first, they can survive anything. It's only when we have such experiences without understanding what they are or why we're having them that we can find ourselves locked into years, or even lifetimes, of a pattern that can literally steal the very things from us that we hold most dear . . . such as life itself.

THE FIFTH MIRROR: REFLECTIONS OF OUR GREATEST ACT OF COMPASSION

> *"Show to me the stone which the builders*
> *have rejected. That one is the cornerstone."*[6]
> — The Gospel of Thomas

In the late 1980s, my office was in a huge multistory building in the foothills of Denver. Although the building was enormous, the end of the Cold War and cutbacks in government spending made it necessary for the company where I worked to "downsize" and consolidate. As other divisions of the company moved into our facility, space was at a premium. I shared my office with another employee, a woman performing a function very different from mine within the department. There was no competition or shared responsibilities, and we quickly became good friends, exchanging stories of our family weekends, friends, and the joys and sorrows of life outside of the company.

One day, we'd just returned from lunch when she retrieved the messages that had come in on her voice mail while we were gone. From the corner of my eye, I saw her become very still and then sit down with a glazed look in her eyes. Her face turned pasty white except for the makeup on her lips and cheeks. After she hung up the phone, I gave her a moment to compose herself, then asked what had happened. She looked at me and began a story that I found sad and at the same time powerful.

A good friend of hers had a young daughter with a much-envied combination of beauty, athletic skills, and artistic talents, each of which she'd cultivated since early childhood. As the girl got older, she searched for a way to combine all of her attributes into a single career and chose to be a fashion model. Her family supported her decision and helped her in whatever way they could to fulfill her dream. As she shopped her portfolio to the ad agencies, she found that many responded with enthusiasm. She had offers of travel, education, and more support than she could have imagined. To everyone looking in from the outside, her life couldn't have seemed better.

On a subtle, almost imperceptible level, however, those who really knew her could see that something was changing. Her enthusiasm was giving way to concern. The agencies she was working with were searching for a certain kind of look in the women they would promote. While this young girl certainly had a unique beauty, it wasn't quite what the agencies wanted in the late '80s. Haunted by what it took to get that special something, the young girl asked her family to help her with a series of cosmetic procedures that she felt would mold her body into what the industry was searching for.

She began with the most obvious enhancements, nips, and tucks. While bringing her closer to her goal, she still didn't have quite the "look" and began even more extreme procedures. Since childhood she'd always had a slight overbite, with her chin and jaw recessed slightly. She agreed to a restructuring that involved breaking and resetting her jaw to create better symmetry. Her mouth had been wired shut for about six weeks while the bones healed, and she'd eaten only liquids during that time. Afterward, the wires were removed, and she did have a beautifully symmetrical face with accentuated cheekbones, and the overbite was gone. Looking at a photograph that my office mate had of her friend's daughter, I personally could see little difference between the before- and after-surgery images.

Having lost weight from weeks of being on a liquid diet, this beautiful young woman began to notice that her body no longer had the V shape that it had before the surgery. The *reality* was that due to her weight loss, her upper body had lost the muscle tone that had given her the "model" proportions. Her perception, however, was that there was a problem that could be surgically remedied, and she underwent a procedure to remove her lower "floating" ribs in order to acquire greater definition and proportion.

The stress from all of her procedures put her body into a tailspin. She discovered that she could no longer control the addition or loss of a pound here and there. Her body was in a "lose-weight" mode and she was losing on a daily basis. By the time her parents recognized what was happening and hospitalized her, it was too late: Attributed to a series of complications rather than any one thing, my office mate's friend had passed away that morning. That was the phone message she received after lunch.

You may know people on a similar path, although hopefully a less extreme one. I use this example to emphasize a point. The young woman in this story had an image of perfection in her mind's eye, and that image became her standard of comparison. She constantly held herself in the shadow of that point of reference, using her mental image as the measure of comparison for her physical appearance. Her beliefs said that she was somehow imperfect the way she was, and that her "imperfections" could be fixed through the miracle of modern technology. What happened to this woman, however, runs much deeper than the procedures used to fix her perceived flaws—it goes directly to the heart of this mirror.

Why did the woman feel that such extremes were necessary for her success? Why did her family and friends support her in her drive for perfection? Why did this young person, already beautiful in her own right, feel so compelled to become something other than who she was from the time of her birth? What fear (or fears) became so powerful in her life that she tried to change her appearance to meet the approval of others? Perhaps an even greater question is: *What can we learn from her experience?* What do we use as our yardstick of comparison? What is the point of reference that we hold ourselves accountable to as we gauge our own successes and failures in life?

THE "IMPERFECTIONS" ARE THE PERFECTION

I often share this story in my workshops. Immediately afterward, I'll ask participants to complete a simple chart, where they evaluate themselves in areas such as educational, romantic, professional, and athletic accomplishments. The rating system is made up of four categories that range from "really good" to "really bad." The key here is that I give them very little time to complete the forms. And I do this for a reason: The actual response on paper is less important than the thinking that goes into it.

Whatever the answers, the reality is that anything less than perfect is a participant judging him- or herself. The only way that people can possibly rate themselves as a success or failure is by comparison to something outside of their experience. As we all know, we are our own toughest critics. For this reason, this mirror is known as our greatest act of compassion. It's about compassion for ourselves—what we are and who we've become.

It's through the mirror of ourselves that we're asked to allow compassionately for the perfection that already exists in each moment of life. This is true regardless of how others see that moment or how it actually turns out. Until we attach a significance of our own making to the outcome, each experience is simply an opportunity to express ourselves . . . nothing more and nothing less.

How would your life be different if you allowed everything you do to be perfect just the way it is, regardless of how it turns out? If everything we do and create is done to the best of our ability, then until we compare it to something else, how can it be anything less than great? If a professional project, relationship, or school assignment doesn't turn out the way that was expected, we can always learn from our experiences and do things differently the next time around. In the Divine Matrix, it's the way we feel about ourselves—our performance, appearance, and achievements—that's mirrored back to us as the reality of our world. With this in mind, the deepest healing of our lives may also become our greatest act of compassion. It's the kindness that we give ourselves.

BEYOND THE MIRRORS

While there are certainly other mirrors that show us even subtler secrets of our truest nature, the ones that I've offered here are the five mirrors that allow our greatest healing in the relationships of life. In this process, we find our truest power as creators in the Divine Matrix. Each mirror is a stepping-stone toward a greater level of personal mastery. Once you know about them, you can't "un-know" them. Once you see them play out in your life, you can't "un-see" them. Each time you recognize one of the mirrors in a particular place in your life, there's a good possibility that you'll find the same pattern playing out in other areas as well.

The control issues that bring up so much emotion with your family at home, for example, may surface with much less intensity while bargaining for a used car with a stranger. The reason it's more moderate is because you probably don't have the same level of intimacy with the salesperson as you do with your family and friends. Although the patterns are less intense, they're still there. And this is the beauty of the holographic pattern of consciousness. The resolution that you find in your relationship with the car dealer, the grocery-store checkout clerk, or the server who brought you a burned dinner at your favorite restaurant will trickle into your relationships at home. It must, because that's the very nature of the hologram. Once a pattern changes in one place, every relationship that holds the same pattern will benefit.

The changes sometimes come to us in the places we least expect. If they didn't, we would probably never get up in the morning and say, "Today I'll tackle the relationships that show me my greatest mirrors of my deepest judgments." We just don't seem to work that way! Instead, our opportunities to heal through our mirrors often come while we're on the way to the mailbox or putting air in the tires of our car.

Not long ago, I met a friend who'd just given up a career, family, friends, and a relationship in another state to move to the wilderness of northern New Mexico. I asked him why he had left so much behind to live in the isolation of the high desert. He began telling me that he'd come to find his "spiritual path." In the same breath, however, he told me that he hadn't been able to get started because nothing was going right. He was having problems with his family, business plans, and even the contractors who were building his new "spiritual" home. His frustration was obvious. Listening to his story, I offered the one insight that I felt might help.

From my perspective, we're incapable of anything other than a spiritual life. To put it another way, as beings of spirit, we're capable only of spiritual experiences. Regardless of what life may look like, I believe that each endeavor and all our paths are leading us to the same place. From that belief, the activities of every day can't be separate *from* our spiritual evolution—they *are* our spiritual evolution!

I turned to my friend and suggested that just perhaps all

of the challenges that were in his life at the moment *were* his spiritual path. While this was obviously not the answer that he'd expected, he was curious about what I meant. He had an idea that his spirituality would be realized by living in solitude and quiet contemplation each day.

I clarified my beliefs, suggesting that although all these things may become part of his life, the way he would resolve each of the challenges facing him could be precisely the path that he'd come to explore. Glancing back at me with a surprised look on his face as we said our good-byes, he simply replied, "Maybe it is!"

CHAPTER EIGHT

REWRITING THE REALITY CODE: 20 KEYS TO CONSCIOUS CREATION

"You have now found the conditions in which the desire of your heart can become the reality of your being. Stay here until you acquire a force in you that nothing can destroy."
— Spoken to the mystic Gurdjieff by his teacher in *Meetings with Remarkable Men: Gurdjieff's Search for Hidden Knowledge*[1]

The words of a popular '70s rock ballad by the group Ten Years After echo the same heartfelt desire that I've heard from people throughout the world who desperately want to make a difference and yet feel helpless to do so. "I'd love to change the world," the chorus begins, "But I don't know what to do / So I'll leave it up to you."[2] My hope is that in the pages that follow, we'll weave together everything we need for the instructions to empower ourselves with the knowledge to create a better world.

In the first chapter of this book, I shared the story of my Native American friend and how the people of his tradition believe that we mysteriously began to forget our power to change the universe long ago. He suggested that the complex technology being used today is our attempt to remember this ability by mimicking in our world what we can actually do in our bodies. With this in mind, it's not surprising that computers have become such an integral part of our lives: They do in fact appear to mimic the way we store our memories and communicate with one another.

The comparison of inner versus outer technology may go even further than my friend suspected, however (or at least further than he shared with me on that day). In many ways, our brains and even consciousness itself have been compared to the way a modern computer works. In his groundbreaking book *Consciousness Explained,* Daniel Dennett, director of the Center for Cognitive Studies at Tufts University, says that we can actually think of our brains "as a computer of sorts," and that doing so gives us a powerful metaphor to understand how we use information.[3] In many ways, the ideas of computer science give us just what we need to find our way in what he calls the *"terra incognita,"* or the unknown land, between what science tells us about the brain and what we experience *through* it. Clearly, the success of the computer as a tool of memory and communication gives us a powerful analogy to help us understand the mystery of consciousness.

Following is a brief description of how a modern computer works. Although tremendously oversimplified, the information is accurate. This simple model will allow us to compare our outer world of hardware and software to the inner workings of consciousness itself. The parallels are fascinating, and the similarity is unmistakable.

To begin with, all computers need only three things to make them useful. Regardless of how big or small or how complicated a computer may look, it will always need *hardware,* an *operating system,* and *software* to perform. So far, this sounds simple enough . . . but to shed a new light on consciousness, it's important to understand just what these three parts of a computer really do.

The operating system is what makes it possible for us to communicate with our computer's chips and circuits, and ultimately make something happen on the printer, screen, and so forth. Whether it's the familiar Macintosh or Windows operating systems, or even the more exotic ones developed for special tasks, when we type our commands into the keyboard, it's because of this operating system that they make sense to the computer. It translates our instructions into something that the machine recognizes.

The hardware is the physical structure of the computer itself. It includes things such as the monitor and keyboard, as well as the circuits, chips, and processors—the gadgets through which the operating system works. The output of a computer's work is typically made visible on some kind of hardware device. In addition to the screen, this may include the printers, plotters, and projectors that display what we've created.

The software includes the familiar programs such as Word, PowerPoint, and Excel that we use every day in our offices and schools to get our jobs done. It's through our interface with these programs that the computer receives the commands from us that make the whole thing useful!

Here's the key to this analogy: For all intents and purposes, the operating system of a computer is fixed and doesn't change. In other words, it "is" what it is. When we want to see our computer do something different, we don't change the operating system—*we change the commands that go into it.* The reason why this is important is that consciousness appears to work in precisely the same way.

If we think of the entire universe as a massive consciousness computer, then consciousness itself is the operating system, and reality is the output. Just as a computer's operating system is fixed and changes must come from the programs that speak to it, in order to change our world, we must alter the programs that make sense to reality: feelings, emotions, prayers, and beliefs.

Function	Electronic Computer	Consciousness Computer
Hardware	CPU, Screen Printer, etc.	Reality (The Divine Matrix)
		↑
Operating System	XP, Windows, Macintosh	Consciousness
		↑
Programs (software)	Word, Excel, PowerPoint	Feelings, Emotions, Prayer, Beliefs

To change our reality, we must change the commands of Feeling, Emotion, Prayer, and Belief that program reality.

Figure 13. A comparison of a consciousness computer and a familiar electronic one: For both, the way to change the output is through the language that the system recognizes.

Key 20: We must become in our lives the very things that we choose to experience in our world.

Everything that we could ever imagine, and probably things that we've never considered, are possible within this mode of seeing ourselves. Just as programs such as Word and Works are the ways that we modify the output of our computer . . . feeling, belief, and prayer are the programs that change the output of consciousness as the Divine Matrix. The beauty of this analogy is that we already have these powerful programs of reality making, and we're already using them every day.

Each moment we're sending our messages of emotion, feeling, prayers, and belief to consciousness, which translates the code of what we send into the daily reality of our bodies, relationships, lives, and world. The question now is less about whether this language exists and more about how intentionally we use it in our lives.

To understand precisely why our beliefs are so powerful and how we make such a difference in a world of six billion or so people, we'll take our understanding of the hologram one step further.

PATTERNS OF THE WHOLE

It should be obvious by now that we're holographic beings. It ought to be equally apparent that we're holographic bodies living in the holographic consciousness of a holographic universe. We're powerful beings expressing ourselves through the bodies that extend beyond the edge of our cells to become the universe itself. By simply "being" who we are, we encompass the whole of creation, mirroring everything from the largest phenomenon to the minutest occurrence, from the lightest of the light to the darkest of the dark. Our friends are part of that whole, as well as our partners, parents, and children. Our bodies mirror the patterns of the universe, embedded within more patterns, embedded within still more patterns, and so on. Our holographic existence is no secret, however, and has been the subject of some of the most profound and moving prose and poetry in the history of our world.

In the Gnostic work *The Thunder: Perfect Mind,* for example, a 3rd-century woman declares that she is nothing more and nothing less than the embodiment of all the possibilities that already exist within every person. "I am the first and the last," she states. "I am the whore and the holy one. I am the wife and the virgin. . . . I am the mother of my father and the sister of my husband. . . . In my weakness, do not forsake me, and do not be afraid of my power. . . . Why have you hated me in your counsels?"[4]

As accurately as these words may describe our holographic existence, they were written during the early years of the Christian church and were far ahead of their time. With this in mind, when the patriarchy of the church council was asked to choose which documents would be omitted from the "official" religious texts, it's easy to see why *The Thunder: Perfect Mind* was lost until the discovery of the pre-church Nag Hammadi library, nearly 1,700 years later.

What's important here is that each of us is whole and complete unto ourselves. And in this state, we find the key to even greater patterns of healing that exist within an even greater wholeness. It's this powerful principle that plays out in our lives, triggering experiences and emotions that may in fact have little to do with what we think they're all about.

For example, there's a good chance that the sadness we feel during a movie depicting loss has very little to do with the actual scene that's portrayed in the movie. The riveting scene of soldiers shooting at the wolf tamed by John Dunbar (played by Kevin Costner) in the 1990 film *Dances with Wolves* is a perfect illustration of how this principle plays out in our lives. We watch through Dunbar's eyes as the same soldiers who have taken him prisoner attack the wolf that has come to trust him as a friend.

I've seen this film on many occasions, and each time, the emotion that this scene elicits from the audience is powerful, genuine—and to some people, a mystery. *Why do we feel so much sadness from seeing the wolf Two Socks hunted and killed?* they ask. The answer might surprise them. The reason is because there's a good possibility that the sadness they feel may have very little to do with what has just happened on the screen. There's a good possibility that within the space of a few minutes, the movie has triggered feelings that they've locked away every time they've lost something precious or had it taken away from them.

Ultimately, it's not surprising to discover that the feelings evoked while watching a film probably have more to do with us—what we've lost within ourselves to survive our experiences of life—than the people who are going through their drama in the movie. Without knowing that we've given so much of ourselves away, however, we may find ourselves reacting to the trigger of books, movies, or situations we identify with. This is our way of reminding ourselves that we still recognize the things that we've lost in order to survive the hurtful moments of life.

Our lives seem to work this way: Each of us reflects for others different pieces of the whole. We're reminded of this in the ancient hermetic principle of "as above, so below; as within, so without." As physicist John Wheeler suggested, we may be like cosmic feedback loops in the universe, with the same pattern repeating itself again and again, on different levels of scale. Taking this idea one step further, ancient traditions suggest that the "experience" loop of life continues for as long as it takes us to find our greatest healing. Then we're released from the cycle—or as Hindu beliefs affirm, our karma is complete.

SOMEONE MUST DO IT FIRST

In the living hologram of our consciousness computer, each and every piece of the hologram, no matter how small, lives within the realm of its own space. As such, it's in service to a greater whole. The subatomic particles, for example, are what the atoms are made of and what determines how they work; the atoms, in turn, make up the molecules and dictate how *they* work; the molecules comprise the cells of our bodies and constitute how *we* work; and our bodies are a mirror of the cosmos . . . and so on.

Precisely because of the nature of a hologram, as we saw in Part II, a change on any level is reflected throughout the whole. Thus, it doesn't take many people to anchor a new way of thinking or believing within the overall pattern of consciousness. From the Native Americans of the 15th century who learned to "see" the anomalous pattern of foreign ships after their tribal healer discovered how to change his sight, to the populations in Israel and Lebanon in the 1980s who experienced peace after individuals trained in a special way to feel peace did so at prescribed times, relatively few people creating a new program in consciousness can make a huge difference in the outcome of our collective reality. The key is that someone must do it first.

One person must choose a new way of being and live that difference in the presence of others so that it can be witnessed and sealed into the pattern. In doing so, we upgrade our programs of belief and send consciousness the blueprint for a new reality. We've seen this principle work many times in our past: From Buddha, Jesus, and Mohammed to Gandhi, Mother Teresa, and Martin Luther King, Jr., numerous individuals lived a new way of being in the presence of others. And they did so within the very consciousness that they chose to change. We may have heard about such powerful examples of change for so long that we take them for granted today.

A closer look at the way these masters have gone about seeding new ideas in an existing paradigm, however, is nothing short of astonishing. If we were to see such a thing in our computer analogy, it would be the equivalent of having our word-processing software suddenly reprogram itself to do rocket science . . . if such a thing happened, it would be the epitome of artificial intelligence! And that's just about how miraculous it is for us to create a great change in the presence of the same beliefs that have limited us in the past.

That's why it's so powerful when we find a way to trust in a universe that gives us good reason to fear, find forgiveness on a planet that's been entrenched in revenge, or find compassion in a world that has learned to kill what is feared or not understood. This is precisely what our master teachers accomplished. By living their wisdom, compassion, trust, and love, visionaries of our past changed the "software" of belief that was speaking to the "operating system" of consciousness. As the seeds of new possibilities, they "upgraded" our reality.

Today we have the same opportunity. We don't have to be saints to make a difference. There's an interesting distinction that makes our current choices different from those of our past. The scientific studies show that the more people there are who embrace a new belief, the easier it is to anchor that belief as a reality. (As mentioned in Part II, the "square root of one percent" equation simply demonstrates how many people it takes to begin the change.) While Buddha, Jesus, and the other masters may have been the first to accomplish what they did, their examples proved to be the catalysts that opened the door for others to do the same. Even Jesus himself suggested that future generations would do what looked miraculous to the people of his day.

There have been many years and many people that have followed the lead of such visionaries, and the momentum of what they offered is the advantage that we have over the visionaries of our past. Today we *know* that we can heal our bodies and live to an advanced age. We *know* that love, appreciation, and gratitude are the life-affirming qualities that infuse our bodies with vitality and our world with peace. And we *know* that with the knowledge to upgrade what we say to the Divine Matrix, relatively few people can make a big difference.

So what do we do with such knowledge? What happens if one person decides on a new response to an old and hurtful pattern? What occurs if someone chooses to respond to "betrayal" or "violated trust," for example, with something other than hurt and anger? What do you think takes place in a family when one member begins to watch the six o'clock news without feeling the need for revenge or to get even with those who have wronged and violated others? What happens is this: That single individual becomes a living bridge—both the pioneer and midwife—for every other person with the courage to choose the same path. Each time someone else makes the same choice, it's a little easier because another person did it first.

As we discovered earlier, the key to their success is that in order to do so, they must *transcend* the things that hurt them without getting lost in the experience. In other words, Martin Luther King, Jr., couldn't bring a stop to hate by hating. Nelson Mandela couldn't have survived more than two decades in a South African prison if he had despised those who imprisoned him. In the same way, it's impossible to end war by creating more wars. We've seen a powerful example of precisely this principle in our inability to find peace in the 20th century. Bottom line: In a universe that mirrors our beliefs, it's clear that angry people can't create a peaceful world.

We've tried, and the instability of the world today is the evidence of where our efforts have led.

In our examples of those who have changed the cycles of oppression from within the oppression itself, two powerful patterns emerge:

1. The choice to see beyond the hate originates from within the same system that spawns it, rather than being imposed upon the system from an outside source.

2. The people who make such a choice become the living bridge for those people they love the most. They find their truest power by living their truth in a system that doesn't support their beliefs at the time.

What a powerful model! Holographic consciousness provides for a change made *anywhere* in the system becoming a change *everywhere* in the system. Even with six billion–plus people now sharing our world, we all benefit to some degree from the choices of peace and healing that are held by just a few. I can say that with certainty because we've witnessed this principle at work. Through our knowledge of the Divine Matrix, we now have everything we need to embrace our power to create and apply what we know to the great challenges of our time.

Whether we're choosing peace in our world or within our families, healing in our loved ones or in ourselves, the principles are precisely the same. In our analogy of the universe as a consciousness computer with feelings, emotions, beliefs, and prayers programming reality, it makes perfect sense that we would have an instruction manual that highlights the steps of reality making. And we do: Through the ages, the most enlightened masters have shared it with us in bits and pieces. The keys in the next section, drawn from their teachings, are designed to lead us step-by-step through the sequence of logic and actions that's been proven to create change.

While there are certainly other keys, this time-tested sequence has been effective during history, as well as in my own experience. For that reason it's offered here as an abbreviated "how-to" manual for upgrading our programs of reality and changing the world.

20 KEYS TO REALITY MAKING

Here are the keys that encapsulate the highlights of this book. Individually, they're interesting. Collectively, they tell a story—*our* story—a reminder of our power to create. The keys may be considered as the software that our consciousness computer uses for reality making . . . our code of change. And as with any code, the keys are in a sequence for a reason. Simply put, just as we need to have all the ingredients in place before we begin to bake a cake, our keys to reality making work only if each step of the process is understood and available to us when we need it.

When I think about understanding these keys, I'm reminded of a powerful sequence of knowledge described in the mysterious third book of the Kabbalah, the *Sepher Yetzirah.* In the step-by-step instruction describing how the universe was made, the book's unknown author invites the reader to consider each step of creation one at a time. In doing so, the reader gives each one the consideration of its own place of power. "Examine with them, / And probe with them," the text says of the ancient instructions. "Make [each] thing stand on its essence."[5]

Similarly, I invite you to consider the following sequence of keys individually. Allow each its own merit as a powerful agent of change. Work with it until it makes sense to you. Together, these steps can become your code for changing the world and yourself.

20 KEYS OF CONSCIOUS CREATION

Key 1: The Divine Matrix is the *container* that holds the universe, the *bridge* between all things, and the *mirror* that shows us what we have created.

Key 2: Everything in our world is connected to everything else.

Key 3: To tap the force of the universe itself, we must see ourselves as *part of* the world rather than *separate from* it.

Key 4: Once something is joined, *it is always connected,* whether it remains physically linked or not.

Key 5: The act of focusing our consciousness is an act of creation. Consciousness creates!

Key 6: We have all the power we need to create all the changes we choose!

Key 7: The focus of our awareness becomes the reality of our world.

Key 8: To simply *say* that we choose a new reality is not enough!

Key 9: Feeling is the language that "speaks" to the Divine Matrix. Feel as though your goal is accomplished and your prayer is already answered.

Key 10: Not just any feeling will do. The ones that create must be without ego and judgment.

Key 11: We must *become* in our lives the things that we choose to *experience* as our world.

Key 12: We are not bound by the laws of physics as we know them today.

Key 13: In a holographic "something," every piece of the something mirrors the whole something.

Key 14: The universally connected hologram of consciousness promises that the instant we create our good wishes and prayers, they are already received at their destination.

Key 15: Through the hologram of consciousness, a little change in our lives is mirrored everywhere in our world.

Key 16: The minimum number of people required to "jump-start" a change in consciousness is the $\sqrt{1\%}$ of a population.

Key 17: The Divine Matrix serves as the mirror in our world of the relationships that we create in our beliefs.

Key 18: The root of our "negative" experiences may be reduced to one of three universal fears (or a combination of them): abandonment, low self-worth, or lack of trust.

Key 19: Our true beliefs are mirrored in our most intimate relationships.

Key 20: We must become in our lives the very things that we choose to experience in our world.

Almost universally, we share a sense that there's more to us than meets the eye. Somewhere deep within the mists of our ancient memory, we know that we have magical and miraculous powers within us. From the time of childhood, we fantasize about our ability to do things that are beyond the realm of reason and logic. And why not? While we're children, we have yet to "learn" the rules that say miracles can't happen in our lives.

The reminders of our miraculous potential are all around us. In Part II, I suggested that the "anomalies" of quantum particles could be something more than simply "strange" and "spooky" behavior. I asked if the freedom that these particles have to move in space-time is really showing us a freedom that might be possible in our lives. Intentionally, I've waited until now to answer that question. Following all of the experiments and research, along with the demonstration of those who have transcended the limits of their own beliefs, I believe that the answer is yes.

If the particles that we're made of can be in instantaneous communication with one another, exist in two places at once, live in the past as well as the future, and even change history through choices in the present, then we can, too. The only difference between those isolated particles and us is that we're made of a lot of them held together by the power of consciousness itself.

The ancient mystics reminded our hearts, and modern experiments have proven to our minds, that the single most powerful force in the universe lives within each of us. And that is the great secret of creation itself: the power to create in the world what we imagine in our beliefs. While it may sound too simple to be true, I believe that the universe works in precisely this way.

When the Sufi poet Rumi observed that we're afraid of our own immortality, maybe he meant that it is actually the power to choose immortality that truly frightens us.

Just as Christopher Logue's initiates in the Introduction discovered that all they needed was a little nudge to get them to fly, perhaps all we require is a little shift to see that we're the architects of our world and our fate, cosmic artists expressing our inner beliefs on the canvas of the universe. If we can remember that we're the art as well as the artist, then perhaps we can also remember that we're the seed of the miracle as well as the miracle itself. If we can make that small shift, then we're already healed in the Divine Matrix.

Keep walking, though there's
no place to get to. Don't try
to see through the distances.
That's not for human beings.
Move within, but don't move
the way fear makes you move.

— Rumi

ACKNOWLEDGMENTS

*T*he *Divine Matrix* is a synthesis of the research, discoveries, and presentations that began with a small living-room audience in Denver, Colorado, in 1986. Since that time, many people have crossed my path and provided the bridge of experience that led to the powerful and empowering message of this book. Often they participated in ways that they are not even aware of! While it would take an entire volume to name everyone individually, these pages are my opportunity to express my thanks to those whose efforts have directly contributed to making this book possible.

I am especially grateful to:

Every one of the really great people at Hay House! I offer my sincere appreciation and many thanks to Louise Hay, Reid Tracy, and Ron Tillinghast for your vision and dedication to the truly extraordinary way of doing business that has become the hallmark of Hay House's success. To Reid Tracy, president and CEO, I send my deepest gratitude for your support and unwavering faith in me and my work. To Jill Kramer, editorial director, many, many thanks for your honest opinions and guidance; for always being there when I call; and for the years of experience that you bring to each of our conversations.

Angela Torrez, my publicist; Alex Freemon, my copy editor; Jacqui Clark, publicity director; Jeannie Liberati, sales director; Margarete Nielsen, marketing director; Nancy Levin, event director; and Rocky George, audio engineer extraordinaire—I couldn't ask for a nicer group of people to work with, or a more dedicated team to support my work! Your excitement and professionalism are unsurpassed, and I'm proud to be a part of all the good things that the Hay House family brings to our world.

To Ned Leavitt, my literary agent: Many thanks for the wisdom and integrity that you bring to each milestone we cross together. Through your guidance in shepherding our books through the

ENDNOTES

20. Malcolm W. Browne, "Signal Travels Farther and Faster Than Light,"
Thomas Jefferson National Accelerator Facility (Newport News, VA) online
newsletter (July 22, 1997). Website: **www.cebaf.gov/news/internet/1997/
spooky.html.**

21. This quotation from the project leader, professor Nicholas Gisin,
is drawn from an article describing the experiment. "Geneva University
Development in Photon Entanglement for Enhanced Encryption Security and
Quantum Computers" (2000). Website: **www.geneva.ch/Entanglement.
htm.**

22. Malcolm W. Browne, "Signal Travels Farther and Faster Than Light."

Chapter 2

1. *The Illuminated Rumi*, Coleman Barks, trans. (New York: Broadway Books,
1997): p. 13.

2. Quoted by Carl Seelig, *Albert Einstein* (Barcelona, Spain: Espasa-Calpe,
2005).

3. John Wheeler, from an interview with Mirjana R. Gearhart of *Cosmic
Search*, vol. 1, no. 4 (1979). Website: **www.bigear.org/vol1no4/wheeler.
htm.**

4. Ibid.

5. Joel R. Primack, a cosmologist at the University of California at Santa
Cruz, "According to the big bang, space itself is expanding. I don't understand:
If space is expanding, into what is it expanding?" an online article from the
"Ask the Experts" section of the *Scientific American* Website: **www.sciam.com**
(posted October 21, 1999). "According to modern cosmological theory, based on
Einstein's General Relativity (our modern theory of gravity), the big bang did
not occur somewhere in space; it occupied the whole of space. Indeed, it created
space."

6. The Rig Veda, as cited in "Hinduism—Hindu Religion: Discussion of
Metaphysics & Philosophy of Hinduism Beliefs & Hindu Gods." Website: **www.
spaceandmotion.com/Philosophy-Hinduism-Hindu.htm.**

7. Ibid.

8. This effect was first reported in Russia: P.P.Gariaev, K.V. Grigor'ev, A.A.
Vasil'ev, V.P. Poponin, and V.A. Shcheglov, "Investigation of the Fluctuation
Dynamics of DNA Solutions by Laser Correlation Spectroscopy," *Bulletin of
the Lebedev Physics Institute*, no. 11–12 (1992): pp. 23–30, as cited by Vladimir
Poponin in an online article "The DNA Phantom Effect: Direct Measurement
of a New Field in the Vacuum Substructure" (Update on DNA Phantom
Effect, March 19, 2002), The Weather Master Website: **www.twm.co.nz/
DNAPhantom.htm.**

9. Ibid.

10. Vladimir Poponin, "The DNA Phantom Effect: Direct Measurement of
a New Field in the Vacuum Substructure," performed the Russian study again
in 1995 under the auspices of the Institute of HeartMath, Research Division,
Boulder Creek, CA.

11. Ibid.

12. Glen Rein, Ph.D., Mike Atkinson, and Rollin McCraty, M.A., "The
Physiological and Psychological Effects of Compassion and Anger," *Journal of
Advancement in Medicine*, vol. 8, no. 2 (Summer 1995): pp. 87–103.

13. Julie Motz, "Everyone an Energy Healer: The Treat V Conference" Santa
Fe, NM, *Advances: The Journal of Mind-Body Health*, vol. 9 (1993).

14. Jeffrey D. Thompson, D.C., B.F.A., online article, "The Secret Life of
Your Cells," Center for Neuroacoustic Research (2000). This article references
the work of Thompson's colleague Dr. Cleve Backster and a book about

Backster's research of the same title. Website: **www.neuroacoustic.org/ articles/articlecells.htm**.

15. The Institute of HeartMath was founded in 1991 as a nonprofit research organization "providing a range of unique services, products, and technologies to boost performance, productivity, health and well-being while dramatically reducing stress." For more information, please visit the Website: **www.HeartMath.com/company/index.html**.

16. Glen Rein, Ph.D., "Effect of Conscious Intention on Human DNA," Proceedings of the International Forum on New Science (Denver, CO: 1996).

17. Glen Rein, Ph.D., and Rollin McCraty, Ph.D., "Structural Changes in Water and DNA Associated with New Physiologically Measurable States," *Journal of Scientific Exploration*, vol. 8, no. 3 (1994): pp. 438–439.

18. Rein, "Effect of Conscious Intention on Human DNA."

19. Elaine Pagels, *The Gnostic Gospels* (New York: Random House, 1979): pp. 50–51.

20. Planck, "Das Wesen der Materie."

PART II
Chapter 3
1. Chief Seattle, "A Message to Washington from Chief Seattle." Website: **www.chiefseattle.com**.

2. From an interview with John Wheeler by Tim Folger, "Does the Universe Exist if We're Not Looking?" *Discover,* vol. 23, no. 6 (June 2002): p. 44.

3. Neville, *The Power of Awareness* (Marina del Rey, CA: DeVorss, 1961): p. 9.

4. Neville, *The Law and the Promise*, p. 57.

5. Neville, *The Power of Awareness*, pp. 103–105.

6. Ibid., p. 10.

7. Ibid.

8. Seelig, *Albert Einstein*.

9. Michio Kaku, *Hyperspace: A Scientific Odyssey Through Parallel Universes, Time Warps, and the 10th Dimension* (New York: Oxford University Press, 1994): p. 263.

10. C. D. Sharma, *A Critical Survey of Indian Philosophy* (Delhi, India: Motilal Banarsidass Publishers, 1992): p. 109.

11. Neville, *The Law and the Promise*, p. 13.

12. "The Gospel of Thomas," translated and introduced by members of the Coptic Gnostic Library Project of the Institute for Antiquity and Christianity (Claremont, CA). From *The Nag Hammadi Library,* James M. Robinson, ed. (San Francisco, CA: HarperSanFrancisco, 1990): p. 137.

13. "John 16:23–24," *Holy Bible: Authorized King James Version* (Grand Rapids, MI: World Publishing, 1989): p. 80.

14. *Prayers of the Cosmos: Meditations on the Aramaic Words of Jesus,* Neil Douglas-Klotz, trans. (San Francisco, CA: HarperSanFrancisco, 1994): pp. 86–87.

15. Amit Goswami, "The Scientific Evidence for God Is Already Here," *Light of Consciousness*, vol. 16, no. 3 (Winter 2004): p. 32.

16. *The Illuminated Rumi*, p. 98.

17. *The Expanded Quotable Einstein*, p. 205.

18. Jack Cohen and Ian Stewart, *The Collapse of Chaos: Discovering Simplicity in a Complex World* (New York: Penguin Books, 1994): p. 191.

19. One of the clearest sources for the mind-body connection was documented in a landmark study by James Blumenthal at Duke University. "Chill Out: It Does the Heart Good," Duke University news release (July 31, 1999) citing the technical study of the relationship between emotional response

and heart health, originally published in the *Journal of Consulting and Clinical Psychology.* Website: **www.dukemednews.org.**

20. A beautiful example of applying what we know about inner peace to a wartime situation is found in the pioneering study done by David W. Orme-Johnson, Charles N. Alexander, John L. Davies, Howard M. Chandler, and Wallace E. Larimore, "International Peace Project in the Middle East," *The Journal of Conflict Resolution*, vol. 32, no. 4, (December 1988): p. 778.

21. "The Gospel of Thomas," *The Nag Hammadi Library*, p. 134.

22. Joan Carroll Cruz, *Mysteries, Marvels, Miracles in the Lives of the Saints* (Rockford, IL: TAN Books and Publishers, 1997).

23. There are a number of accounts of the miraculous life of Padre Pio that include prophecy, miraculous scents, stigmata, and bilocation. The best source that I could find for this particular account during World War II is the Eternal Word Television Network Website: **www.ewtn.com/padrepio/mystic/bilocation.htm.**

Chapter 4

1. Holographic technology was invented in 1948 by Hungarian scientist Dennis Gabor. In 1971, Gabor was awarded the Nobel Prize in physics for the discovery that he made 23 years earlier.

2. Russell Targ in a special-features commentary with the producers of the 2004 motion picture *Suspect Zero*, directed by E. Elias Merhige (Paramount Studios, DVD release April 2005).

3. Ibid.

4. Ervin Laszlo, "New Concepts of Matter, Life and Mind," a paper published with permission by Physlink at the Website: **www.physlink.com/Education/essay_laszlo.cfm.**

5. Francis Harold Cook, *Hua-yen Buddhism*, p. 2.

6. Ibid.

7. Laszlo, "New Concepts of Matter, Life and Mind."

8. Karl Pribram, as quoted in an interview by Daniel Goleman, "Pribram: The Magellan of Brain Science," on the SyberVision Website: **www.sybervision.com/Golf/hologram.htm.**

9. Ibid.

10. "International Peace Project in the Middle East," *The Journal of Conflict Resolution*, p. 778.

11. "Matthew 17:20," *The New Jerusalem Bible: The Complete Text of the Ancient Canon of the Scriptures*, Standard Edition, Henry Wansbrough, ed. (New York: Doubleday, 1998): p. 1129.

12. Neville, *The Power of Awareness*, p. 118.

13. *101 Miracles of Natural Healing*, an instructional video in the step-by-step methods of the Chi-Lel™ method of healing created by founder Dr. Pang Ming. Website: **www.chilel-qigong.com.**

14. Neville, *The Power of Awareness*, p. 10.

Chapter 5

1. *The Expanded Quotable Einstein*, p. 75.

2. Yitta Halberstam and Judith Leventhal, *Small Miracles: Extraordinary Coincidences From Everyday Life* (Avon, MA: Adams Media Corporation, 1997).

3. Jim Schnabel, *Remote Viewers: The Secret History of America's Psychic Spies* (New York: Bantam Doubleday Dell, 1997): pp. 12–13.

4. Russell Targ, from *Suspect Zero* DVD.

5. Jim Schnabel, *Remote Viewers*, p. 380.

6. Benjamin Lee Whorf, *Language, Thought, and Reality*, John B. Carroll, ed.

(Cambridge, MA: MIT Press, 1964): pp. 58–59.
7. Ibid., p. 262.
8. Ibid.
9. Ibid., p. 59.
10. "Mathematical Foundations of Quantum Theory: Proceedings of the New Orleans Conference on the Mathematical Foundations of Quantum Theory," *Quantum Theory and Measurement*, J. A. Wheeler and W. H. Zurek, eds. (Princeton, NJ: Princeton University Press, 1983): pp. 182–213.
11. Yoon-Ho Kim, R. Yu, S.P. Kulik, Y.H. Shih, and Marlan O. Scully, "Delayed 'Choice' Quantum Eraser," *Physical Review Letters*, vol. 84, no. 1 (2000): pp. 1–5.

PART III

Chapter 6

1. Carlos Castaneda, *Journey to Ixtlan: The Lessons of Don Juan* (New York: Washington Square Press, 1972): p. 61.
2. Douglas-Klotz, *Prayers of the Cosmos*, p. 12.
3. Gregg Braden, *The God Code: The Secret of Our Past, the Promise of Our Future* (Carlsbad, CA: Hay House, 2005), p. xv.

Chapter 7

1. Ernest Holmes, *The Science of Mind* (from the original 1926 version, Part IID, Lesson Four: Recapitulation). Website: **ernestholmes.wwwhubs.com/sompart2d.htm**.
2. "The Gospel of Thomas," *The Nag Hammadi Library*, p. 136.
3. Ibid., p. 126.
4. Ibid, p. 136.
5. Ibid, p. 134.
6. Ibid.

Chapter 8

1. *Meetings with Remarkable Men: Gurdjieff's Search for Hidden Knowledge* (Corinth Video, 1987). This motion picture is based on the life of Gurdjieff and his relentless search to know the secret teachings of the past. His travels led him throughout the world and ultimately to a secret monastery believed to be located in the remote wilderness of mountainous Pakistan. These are the words that his teacher offered to him as he attained the mastership that he had searched for for so long.
2. Ten Years After, from their album *A Space In Time* (Capitol Records, 1971).
3. Daniel Dennett, *Consciousness Explained* (Boston: Back Bay Books, 1991): p. 433.
4. "The Thunder: Perfect Mind," *The Nag Hammadi Library*, pp. 297–303.
5. *Sefer Yetzirah: The Book of Creation*, Aryeh Kaplan, ed. (York Beach, ME: Samuel Weiser, 1997): p. 165.

INDEX

ABOUT THE AUTHOR

New York Times best-selling author **Gregg Braden** has been a featured guest for international conferences and media specials, exploring the role of spirituality in technology. A former senior computer systems designer (Martin Marietta Aerospace), computer geologist (Phillips Petroleum), and technical operations manager (Cisco Systems), Gregg is considered a leading authority on bridging the wisdom of our past with the science, healing, and peace of our future.

For more than 20 years, Gregg has searched high mountain villages, remote monasteries, ancient temples, and forgotten texts to uncover their timeless secrets. His search led to the 2004 release of his paradigm-shattering book *The God Code*, revealing the actual words of an ancient message coded into the DNA of all life.

Between 1998 and 2005, Gregg's journeys into the monasteries of central Tibet revealed a forgotten form of prayer that was lost during the biblical edits of the early Christian church. In his 2006 release, *Secrets of the Lost Mode of Prayer*, he documents this mode of prayer that has no words or outward expression, yet gives us direct access to the quantum force that connects all things.

From his groundbreaking book *Awakening to Zero Point*, to the intimacy of *Walking Between the Worlds* and the controversy of *The Isaiah Effect*, Gregg's work awakens the best in each of us, inspiring our deepest passions with the tools to build a better world.

For further information, please contact Gregg's office at:

Wisdom Traditions
P.O. Box 5182
Santa Fe, New Mexico 87502
(505) 424-6892
Website: **www.greggbraden.com**
E-mail: ssawbraden@aol.com

NOTES

NOTES

Hay House Titles of Related Interest

Divine Magic: The Seven Sacred Secrets of Manifestion,
revised and edited by Doreen Virtue, Ph.D.

Everything You Need to Know to Feel Go(o)d,
by Candace B. Pert, Ph.D., with Nancy Marriott

Exploring the Levels of Creation, by Sylvia Browne

The Four Insights: Wisdom, Power, and
Grace of the Earthkeepers, by Alberto Villoldo, Ph.D.

Love Thyself: *The Message from Water III,*
by Masaru Emoto

Quantum Success: The Astounding Science of
Wealth and Happiness, by Sandra Anne Taylor

What Happens When We Die: *A Groundbreaking*
Study into the Nature of Life and Death, by Sam Parnia, M.D.

Your Immortal Reality: How to Break the Cycle
of Birth and Death, by Gary R. Renard

All of the above are available at your local bookstore,
or may be ordered by contacting Hay House (see next page).

We hope you enjoyed this Hay House book.
If you'd like to receive a free catalog featuring additional
Hay House books and products, or if you'd like information
about the Hay Foundation, please contact:

Hay House, Inc.
P.O. Box 5100
Carlsbad, CA 92018-5100

(760) 431-7695 or (800) 654-5126
(760) 431-6948 (fax) or (800) 650-5115 (fax)
www.hayhouse.com® • www.hayfoundation.org

Published and distributed in Australia by: Hay House Australia Pty. Ltd. •
18/36 Ralph St. • Alexandria NSW 2015 • *Phone:* 612-9669-4299
Fax: 612-9669-4144 • www.hayhouse.com.au

Published and distributed in the United Kingdom by: Hay House UK,
Ltd. • 292B Kensal Rd., London W10 5BE • *Phone:* 44-20-8962-1230
Fax: 44-20-8962-1239 • www.hayhouse.co.uk

Published and distributed in the Republic of South Africa by:
Hay House SA (Pty), Ltd., P.O. Box 990, Witkoppen 2068
Phone/Fax: 27-11-706-6612 • orders@psdprom.co.za

Published in India by: Hay House Publications (India) Pvt. Ltd.,
Muskaan Complex, Plot No. 3, B-2, Vasant Kunj, New Delhi 110 070
Phone: 91-11-4176-1620 • *Fax:* 91-11-4176-1630 • www.hayhouseindia.co.in

Distributed in Canada by: Raincoast • 9050 Shaughnessy St., Vancouver,
B.C. V6P 6E5 • *Phone:* (604) 323-7100 • *Fax:* (604) 323-2600
www.raincoast.com

Tune in to **HayHouseRadio.com**® for the best in inspirational talk radio
featuring top Hay House authors! And, sign up via the Hay House USA Website
to receive the Hay House online newsletter and stay informed about what's
going on with your favorite authors. You'll receive bimonthly announcements
about: Discounts and Offers, Special Events, Product Highlights, Free Excerpts,
Giveaways, and more! www.**hayhouse.com**®

Tune in to Hay House Radio to listen to your favorite authors: **HayHouseRadio.com**®

Yes, I'd like to receive:

☐ **a Hay House catalog**   ☐ *The Louise Hay Newsletter*
☐ *The Christiane Northrup Newsletter*   ☐ *The Sylvia Browne Newsletter*

Name_____

Address_____

City_____ State_____ Zip_____

E-mail_____

Also, please send:

☐ **a Hay House catalog**   ☐ *The Louise Hay Newsletter*
☐ *The Christiane Northrup Newsletter*   ☐ *The Sylvia Browne Newsletter*

To:
Name_____

Address_____

City_____ State_____ Zip_____

E-mail_____

If you'd like to receive a catalog of Hay House books
and products, or a free copy of one or more of our authors'
newsletters, please visit **www.hayhouse.com**® or detach
and mail this reply card.

To:

HAY HOUSE, INC.
P.O. Box 5100
Carlsbad, CA 92018-5100

publishing world, we have reached more people than ever before with our empowering message of hope and possibility. While I deeply appreciate your impeccable guidance, I am especially grateful for your friendship and your trust.

Stephanie Gunning, my first-line editor and friend . . . many thanks for your dedication and skill, and for the energy that you embody in all that you do. Most of all, thank you for helping me to take the complexities of science and find the words to share them in a joyous and meaningful way. I am amazed at how you always ask just the right questions, in just the right way, to lead to the clearest choices.

I am proud to be part of the virtual team, and the family, that has grown around the support of my work over the years, including Lauri Willmot, my favorite (and only) office manager. You have my admiration and countless thanks for being there always—and especially when it counts! To Robin and Jerry Miner of Sourcebooks, many thanks for sticking with us over the years and for creating great events and such a beautiful presentation of the material that supports our programs. To M.A. Bjarkman, Rae Baskin, Sharon Krieg, Vick Spaulding, and everyone at The Conference Works! . . . my deepest gratitude for all that you do to help us share our message with such beautiful audiences throughout the country.

To my mother, Sylvia; and my brother, Eric . . . thank you for your unfailing love and for believing in me. Although our family by blood is small, together we have found that our extended family of love is greater than we ever imagined. My gratitude for all that you bring to each day of my life extends beyond any words that I could possibly write on this page. Eric, audio/visual engineer and technical guru extraordinaire, a very special thank-you for your patience with the many, varied, and often challenging venues that we find ourselves working in. While I am proud to share our work together, I am especially proud to be your brother in life.

To the one person who sees me at my very best, and my very worst, Kennedy, my beloved wife and partner in life. Thank you for your ever-present love and unwavering support, and for your patience with our long days, short nights, and long-distance good

mornings. Most of all, thank you for all that you do to keep us strong and healthy, and for helping me keep my promise to be at my best, always! Your words of encouragement always come at just the right time, and in ways that you could never know!

A very special thanks to everyone who has supported our work, books, recordings, and live presentations over the years. I am honored by your trust and in awe of your vision for a better world. Through your presence, I have learned to become a better listener, and heard the words that allow me to share our empowering message of hope and possibility. To all, I remain grateful always.

ENDNOTES

Introduction

1. "Come to the Edge" is a poem by Christopher Logue written in 1968 for a festival in honor of the 50th anniversary of the death of the French poet Guillaume Apollinaire. The poem is found in Christopher Logue, *Ode to the Dodo: Poems from 1953 to 1978* (London: Jonathan Cape, 1981): p. 96.

2. *The Expanded Quotable Einstein*, Alice Calaprice, ed. (Princeton, NJ: Princeton University Press, 2000): p. 220.

3. John Wheeler, as quoted by F. David Peat in *Synchronicity: The Bridge Between Matter and Mind* (New York: Bantam Books, 1987): p. 4.

4. David Bohm and F. David Peat, *Science, Order, and Creativity* (New York: Bantam Books, 1987): p. 88.

5. David Bohm, *Wholeness and the Implicate Order* (London: Routledge & Kegan Paul, 1980): p. 62.

6. Ibid.

7. Ibid., p. 14.

8. Michael Wise, Martin Abegg, Jr., and Edward Cook, *The Dead Sea Scrolls: A New Translation* (San Francisco, CA: HarperSanFrancisco, 1996): p. 365.

9. Glen Rein, Ph.D., Mike Atkinson, and Rollin McCraty, M.A., "The Physiological and Psychological Effects of Compassion and Anger," *Journal of Advancement in Medicine,* vol. 8, no. 2 (1995): pp. 87–103.

10. The ancient Vedic traditions suggest that the unified field of energy is an infinite field of energy that underlies the infinitely diverse universe. Website: **www.vedicknowledge.com**.

11. The ancient *Hsin-Hsin Ming* (Verses on the Faith Mind) is attributed to Chien Chih Seng-ts'an, third Zen patriarch, in the 6th century. This particular quote is from the English translation by Richard B. Clarke and illustrated by Gyoskusei Jikihara, *Hsin-Hsin Ming: Seng-ts'an Third Zen Patriarch* (Buffalo, NY: White Pine Press, 2001).

12. Ibid.

PART 1
Chapter 1

1. Dean Radin in a special-features commentary with the producers of the 2004 motion picture *Suspect Zero*, directed by E. Elias Merhige (Paramount Studios, DVD release April 2005). The plot of the movie revolves around the use of remote viewing for criminal investigation. For 15 years, Radin has conducted experimental studies of psi phenomena in academia and industry, through his appointments at institutions that include Princeton University, the University of Edinburgh, the University of Nevada, and SRI International. He is currently a senior scientist with the Institute of Noetic Sciences, an organization whose charter it is to explore "the frontiers of consciousness to advance individual, social, and global transformation."

2. Neville, *The Law and the Promise* (Marina del Rey, CA: DeVorss, 1961): p. 9.

3. Ibid., p. 44.

4. *The Expanded Quotable Einstein*, p. 75.

5. Francis Harold Cook, *Hua-yen Buddhism: The Jewel Net of Indra* (University Park, PA: Pennsylvania State University Press, 1977): p. 2.

6. James Clerk Maxwell, "father" of electromagnetic theory. This quote opens the article that he was asked to write on the ether field for the ninth edition of *Encyclopedia Britannica*, issued by Cambridge University Press in 1890. Website: **www.mathpages.com/home/kmath322/kmath322.htm**.

7. Spoken by physicist Hendrik Lorentz in 1906 and quoted in an online collection of viewpoints about the ether field, "Physics—On Absolute Space (Aether, Ether, Akasa) and Its Properties as an Infinite Eternal Continuous Wave Medium." Website: **www.spaceandmotion.com/Physics-Space-Aether-Ether.htm**.

8. Spoken by Albert Einstein during a lecture in 1928. Ibid.

9. Ibid.

10. A. A. Michelson, "The Relative Motion of the Earth and the Luminiferous Ether," *American Journal of Science,* vol. 22 (1881): pp. 120–129.

11. A. A. Michelson and Edward W. Morley, "On the Relative Motion of the Earth and the Luminiferous Ether," *American Journal of Science,* vol. 34 (1887): pp. 333–345.

12. E. W. Silvertooth, "Special Relativity," *Nature,* vol. 322 (14 August 1986): p. 590.

13. Konrad Finagle, *What's the Void?* (Barney Noble, 1898) [Excerpts reprinted in D. E. Simanek and J. C. Holden, *Science Askew* (Boca Raton, FL: Institute of Physics Publishing, 2002)]. Website: **www.lhup.edu/~dsimanek/cutting/grav.htm**.

14. Spoken by Albert Einstein during a lecture in 1928. "Physics—On Absolute Space (Aether, Ether, Akasa) and Its Properties as an Infinite Eternal Continuous Wave Medium."

15. Max Planck, from a speech that he gave in Florence, Italy, in 1944, entitled: "Das Wesen der Materie" (The Essence/Nature/Character of Matter). Source: Archiv zur Geschichte der Max-Planck-Gesellschaft, Abt. Va, Rep. 11 Planck, Nr. 1797.

Below I have included a portion of that speech in the original German, with the English translation following.

Original German: "Als Physiker, der sein ganzes Leben der nüchternen Wissenschaft, der Erforschung der Materie widmete, bin ich sicher von dem Verdacht frei, für einen Schwarmgeist gehalten zu werden. Und so sage ich nach meinen Erforschungen des Atoms dieses: Es gibt keine Materie an sich. Alle Materie entsteht und besteht nur durch eine Kraft, welche die Atomteilchen in Schwingung bringt und sie zum winzigsten Sonnensystem des Alls zusammenhält. Da es im ganzen Weltall aber weder eine intelligente Kraft noch eine ewige Kraft gibt - es ist der Menschheit nicht gelungen, das heißersehnte Perpetuum mobile zu erfinden - so müssen wir hinter dieser Kraft einen *bewußten intelligenten Geist* annehmen. Dieser Geist ist der Urgrund aller Materie."

English Translation: "As a man who has devoted his whole life to the most clear-headed science, to the study of matter, I can tell you as a result of my research about the atoms this much: There is no matter as such! All matter originates and exists only by virtue of a force which brings the particles of an atom to vibration and holds this most minute solar system of the atom together. . . . We must assume behind this force the existence of a conscious and intelligent Mind. This Mind is the matrix of all matter."

16. Albert Einstein, quoted by physicist Michio Kaku in an online article, "M-Theory: The Mother of all SuperStrings: An introduction to M-Theory" (2005). Website: **www.mkaku.org/article_mtheory.htm**.

17. *The Expanded Quotable Einstein,* p. 204.

18. Zhi Zhao, Yu-Ao Chen, An-Ning Zhang, Tao Yang, Hans J. Briegel, and Jian-Wei Pan, "Experimental Demonstration of Five-photon entanglement and Open-destination Teleportation," *Nature,* vol. 430 (2004): p. 54.

19. Eric Smalley, "Five Photons Linked," *Technology Research News* (August/September 2004). Website: **www.trnmag.com/Stories/2004/082504/Five_photons_linked_082504.html**.